A WORLD WITHOUT WAR

ESSAYS

*

A WORLD WITHOUT WAR

ESSAYS

*

D.R. THOMPSON

—DEL SOL PRESS • WASHINGTON D. C.—

A World Without War: Essays by D.R. Thompson
All material © Donald Raymond Thompson, 2012

DEL SOL PRESS, WASHINGTON, D. C.
www.webdelsol.com

This is a first edition.
Ebook ISBN: 978-1-937572-25-29
Print ISBN: 978-1-934832-14-1

All Rights Reserved. Printed in the United States of America. No part of this book may be reproduced in any manner whatsoever without the written permission of the author, except in the case of brief quotations embodied in critical articles and reviews. For information please go to <www.webdelsol.com>.

CONTENTS

Preface   xiii

THE NEW MEDIA AGE (2000)   15
IS BIG MEDIA THE ANTI-CHRIST? (2003)   23
CARTOON NATION (2004)   29
LAND OF THE FREE, HOME OF THE WIMPS (2004)   35
PEACE AS STYLE (2004)   41
LIBERAL WARFARE STATE (2005)   47
THE RULE OF CAPITAL (2006)   53
LOVING PARANOID MEDIA (2006)   63
LONGING FOR MAYBERRY (2007)   71
THERE WILL BE BUCKS (2007)   79
EMERSON MEETS WALL STREET (2009)   89
SUFFOCATING THE DREAM (2010)   99
TIME FOR EXOPOLITICS? (2010)   103
JUDGMENT AT NUREMBERG (2010)   109
DIGITAL MORALITY (2011)   115
THE TREE OF LIFE (2011)   119
A NEW HUMANISM (2011)   127
WAKE UP TIME FOR AMERICA (Spring, 2011)   135
A WORLD WITHOUT WAR (2006)   143

Acknowledgments   149
About D.R. Thompson   151

To a better world…

"Love and compassion are necessities, not luxuries.
Without them humanity cannot survive."

—The Dalai Lama

A REVOLUTION IN PERCEPTION

The globalization of media and the proliferation of telecommunications will allow for a break on the hold of traditional media and the view that it purports. Media will become universal and democratic. Many points of view, hundreds or even thousands of points of view, will all be given equal weight. In this new landscape, the information consumer will pick and choose among the vast landscape of information, brought to them through agent software that reflects their very personal perspective.

Neither the State nor the Networks in the name of Democracy will control media content. The whole situation is a floodgate of awareness, because the implications of hundreds or thousands of perspectives being simultaneously available are the seeds of a revolution in perception. That is, the viewer becomes a powerful editor of their own reality. Responsibility for perception shifts from media owners to media perceivers. In turn, the perceivers themselves may add to the overall mix of media, through an increasingly powerful public access infrastructure.

The whole situation will call into question the current media power structures. Technical expertise and understanding of how to create "commercial" media will be in many ways usurped by the ability to resonate powerful truths above the mass of mere information. Media manipulation will become increasingly easy to perceive, call in to question, and address. There will be no secrets anymore, unless we want them because we fear the responsibility of self-awareness. On the other hand, truth will be harder to decipher, and more valuable when it is found.

—Don Thompson describing "The Digital Tribe" (1993)

PREFACE

I began writing essays in earnest for the Internet around 2000; in 2002, Michael Neff (founder of WebDelSol.com) and I agreed to start the *SolPix* webzine. Later, Mike also asked me to contribute to *The Potomac Journal*, and I began to do so on a regular basis. This book is a compilation of essays from those two webzines, with a few more recent blog posts thrown in for good measure.

What I have found so fascinating about publishing ideas on the net is the viral nature of the web and how the seed of an idea can propagate. Now mind you, in no way shape or form am I trying to take credit for all (or even most) of the ideas expressed in this compilation. But I will say that there has been a group of bloggers and essayists on the Internet—myself included—who have helped to change the conversation about a variety of subjects that the mainstream media would not initially touch. It's humbling to find that some of the ideas you express make their way eventually into the mainstream and into the wider public conversation. It's even more humbling when you're never sure of the "source" of these ideas—for there seems to be an organic, living evolution of ideas on the net that transcends any individual. The nature of this organic evolution of ideas on the Internet has yet, as far as I know, to be explored adequately by any intellectual out there.

Suffice it to say that what fueled my own writing, and that of others, was a frustration with the state of public discourse in the mainstream media, all in tandem with a rapidly deteriorating world situation. It is patently obvious to most that the mainstream media has, and continues to be, reflective of ideas and values that are conservative in the truest sense—that is, attempting at all costs to hold together a status quo paradigm even as that paradigm is shifting (or even collapsing) under their feet. Do I blame anyone for this conservatism? Not necessarily. I would probably do the same if I wasn't such an outsider by choice and proclivity.

Cable channels like Russia Today (RT) are in some ways taking up the slack for a lack of "progressive" media so that we can at least be pleased that some alternative ideas are getting out there on the airwaves. But notably RT is funded by interests outside the U.S. that are themselves capable of being co-opted, should those interests be compromised. For example, once the disputed elections of 2011 were completed in Russia, RT's reporting on the topic certainly seemed protective of the Putin regime (although some could argue that RT did report in a balanced way).

But many of us within the Internet diaspora have no agenda beyond our own desire to influence in a positive sense. As such, I'm not "inside," and others on the Internet diaspora aren't either. That said, the evolving alternative political paradigm organically arising on the Internet still splits along two distinct lines that indicate the oppositional mindset that has blinded us for so long still has a great hold on our society. These two general trends are a kind of nostalgia for the past that believes if we just let capitalism "work as it should" all will be well and we can go back to our forefathers' way of doing business. I'll put the libertarians like Ron Paul in that camp, and they seem to be gaining a lot of popularity. The other camp, I'll call Economic Democrats, who believe that government has a place in the New Economy, and also that working people have a place in the boardroom. While I would place myself (for the most part) in this latter group, as would likely many in the Green Party, I believe all the ideas on the left, right or middle need to be vetted through a rigorous methodology (I'll discuss that in a minute). My hope is that libertarians, Greens, Economic Democrats and progressives can form the coalition within which we can move forward. A difficult task, but in my mind there is much we all have in common.

Most likely some will apply to many of the ideas in this book the label of being too "unrealistic" or "socialistic." That said, it has been the agenda of the right to label anything left of Newt Gingrich as "socialistic." Using this argument, Richard Nixon was very much the socialist. It shows how far to the right we have gone in this country—and let's give credit where credit is due—the conservative think tanks and spinmeisters have done a great job over the last 30 years of prodding the country to slowly ebb in a more right-leaning direction.

While I'm admittedly a card-carrying Democrat and social progressive, I try to be practical in my thinking and understand that a strictly partisan approach will not allow us to find solutions for the future. We must all cooperate. For me, I try to find common ground by applying the kind of rigorous critical thinking to the issues along the lines that I learned through my critical studies program at UCLA. That said, certainly many, if not most, of the ideas included in this book are not, and will not, be accepted as practical by mainstream Democrats or Republicans—not accepted at least until another Financial Meltdown-level crisis (or series of them) is at hand.

Since leaving college, I have also spent a significant amount of time in the technology field helping companies optimize their computer environments and improve their systems performance. I even wrote a nationally publicized book about the subject of how to reorganize and optimize computer systems, architecture and infrastructure that launched me into a long career in the field. Along my technological travels, I have been exposed to systems thinkers that are strikingly non-partisan in their view of life. I firmly believe that it is by vetting ideas through a non-partisan system's model—similar in many ways to the kind of analysis we apply to a company's computer processes—that we can find the optimal path to solving our economic and other ills. I believe that many in the Green Party would also agree with that statement. That said, I still go back to the critical framework taught to me at university, as it allows for an intuitive insight that can sometimes be missed in a technical analysis.

With that in mind, I believe the current direction of technology and society, should one ponder it a bit, is more apt to misuse technology than to wield it properly for the common good. I believe in many ways the élites are using technology to lead us toward a kind of techno-slavery in a world primarily run by major corporations. This world, designed to benefit very few people, is nonetheless well in progress. I believe it is a world view that will lead to continued mass misery and environmental collapse.

One reason for the tension between how technology *can* be used and how it is used is that the foundational ideas of this country are rarely factored into the economic sphere—particularly in our financial infrastructure. Instead you find a casino mentality that winds up in blatant misuse of technology, with but one example being the abuse of High Frequency Trading, to the point where some established companies are going on record against the practice. Fortunately, there are examples where the country's ideals *are* reflected (at least for now), such as the Internet, Public Aviation and the Interstate Highway system, all of which blend public and private good. At the end of this preface I have included a "foundational framework" diagram that shows how systems thinking can incorporate the ideals of the Constitution as a starting place for creating any systems model for the economy of the future. Without incorporating our values into our financial infrastructure, we end up being slaves to financial tyranny and/or abusive behavior.

But we're a long way from this framework; rather what we see evolving is authoritarian capitalism, where Big Government and Big Business work in a lockstep agenda that is often out of touch with common human needs (often called the "New World Order" by conspiracy theorists). However, we do have an alternative. That is, to do the right thing. In other words, what we all know in our hearts and minds is correct and rational. For those that believe otherwise, I suggest a healthy dose of reasoned debate. To paraphrase Winston Churchill, people tend to do the correct thing once all other alternatives are exhausted.

But a little recognition of our ills, a little diagnosing is also in order before embarking on solutions. Like an alcoholic, we need to admit to our problems and face them head on. In the spirit of social critique I've included the essays "Is Big Media The Anti-Christ?," "Cartoon Nation," "Peace as Style," "Loving Paranoid Media," "Digital Morality" and pieces regarding the films *There Will Be Blood* and *The Tree of Life*.

At some point, depending on how deep we need and/or want to go into how our history has been distorted and misrepresented, we will need some kind of Truth and Reconciliation Committee, broadcast on C-Span for all to see and probably dealing with multiple subjects at once. The essay about the film *Judgment at Nuremberg* deals with this topic.

Once sobered up and given the truth, any clear-headed individual will understand we need to rethink and reinvent our corrupted economic system and compel international finance to function under the rule of law. Former Labor Secretary Robert Reich has outlined several practical steps that can be taken, including raising taxes on the wealthy (including capital gains), taxing financial transactions, re-instating the Glass Steagall Act to separate investment and commercial banking, breaking up the largest banks, and instituting massive mortgage modifications. But all of these laudable suggestions may still not get us where we need to be.

To move beyond Professor Reich's suggestions, first on any rational agenda must be debt forgiveness. That means, at a minimum, student-debt forgiveness. Following closely there should be mortgage principal reductions and/or restructurings, as suggested by Reich. We also need sovereign-debt forgiveness and/or substantial restructurings. Finally, and most importantly, we need a new currency regime that allows for a non-debt based currency similar to what (in most recent memory) was accomplished by John Kennedy with "United States Notes" that were printed by the Treasury Department and not tied to Federal Reserve debt. Former Canadian Defense Minister Paul Hellyer outlines effectively how to do this in his book *Light at the End of the Tunnel*. Under Hellyer's example, we would unwind our national debt by introducing non-debt money at a certain percentage of the Gross National Product, in tandem with the abolition/nationalization of the Federal Reserve while allowing re-regulated private commercial banks to continue. Like Hellyer's book, the essays "The Rule of Capital," "Emerson Meets Wall Street," "Suffocating the Dream" and "Wake up Time for America" outline why these kinds of policies are necessary today.

Once we have non-debt based currency in the United States (and likely a new world currency regime backed by real assets and complemented by Internet bartering and/or alternative currencies) we need to address environmental issues in an extremely aggressive way. We need an international Manhattan project that ties our new financial system and economic growth to "growing" out of our current environmental crisis through the use of new energy technologies. And even if science determines that "climate change" is natural and all of our climate scientists are wrong, then we should still consider new energy and environmental technologies for economic, aesthetic and health reasons. This effort is alluded to in the essay "Wake up Time for America."

We also need a citizen's dividend or basic income guarantee that complements an intelligently reformed health care system and can empower people to be freer and more creative, and at the same time simplify certain aspects of our social safety net. Again, Robert Reich has supported a similar idea (as did conservative economist Milton Friedman!) in terms of a *reverse income tax*, where the government not only cuts taxes for the poor, but provides supplemental income. This idea is in fact merely an extension of the earned income tax credit (EITC) program already in place.

A citizen's dividend would be different from the EITC or reverse income tax in that it would include the middle class as well; in fact, some would argue that a citizen's dividend should require no means test and be provided to all, thus protecting it from political agendas. This citizen's dividend could be funded by non-debt based money and/or new financial transaction taxes, and is discussed in the essay "Emerson Meets Wall Street."

To maintain a legitimate flow of information and diversity of opinions, we need to liberate the media from big money interests by publicly funding more alternatives and/or breaking up current media oligopolies—something media mogul Ted Turner has gone on record supporting. While many in "traditional media" believe that the Internet has eliminated any requirement for big media break-ups, large media conglomerates do, nonetheless, still exert undue control over a substantial amount of media messaging in this country, and in often in a very limited, top-down way. "Is Big Media the Anti-Christ?" and "The New Media Age" compares Old Media with New Media and shows how change is taking place and needs to continue.

We must re-assert the principle that law enforcement serves the people and their defense, and is not for some other requirements outside of the public domain. "Longing for Mayberry" explores this idea.

I believe we need to realign all national militaries to democratic values and to restore our National Guard to their original mission. In tandem, each individual can accept responsibility for creating a world conducive to peace. "A World Without War" and "Longing for Mayberry" discuss these ideas.

Finally, we need to rediscover our humanity. Human beings are unique, gifted, intelligent, resilient and much better than most in power would have us believe. We need to re-assert our humanity and as a result take control of our institutions to forge them under a set of common values that recognize that people, environment, family, safety, industriousness, entrepreneurship, sportsmanship, and the like, are common to all people and must all come first. All of the essays have at their core the need to nurture our common humanity, not destroy it. Specifically, "A New Humanism" explores how the term "humanism" is changing and how media and culture can evolve in a way that brings people together under the umbrella of common values. From a personal perspective, the overall evolution of the *tone* of the essays over the years hopefully shows a tendency to move away from confrontation and toward reconciliation. In other words, if I'm not attempting or displaying any personal growth, then there's really no point in reading on.

Libertarians should take particular note of any discussion regarding values within this book, for if there is any hope of eventually downsizing government significantly, we need to shift our value system so that the profit motive and self-interest are tempered by "the golden rule," compassion and common decency. In other words, the rule of law and common ethics must be embedded in the individual, and done so both through the family and the educational system. The educated, enlightened and ethical individual can then be the foundation for any libertarian shift.

Possibly the most controversial essay is about Exopolitics. But I will say that based on concrete whistleblower testimony over the last 10 years, for any government official to say things such as "We have no credible evidence of extra-terrestrial life" (the continued stance of the Obama administration) is incredibly insulting to the intelligence of millions, if not billions, around this world who all know very well that parts of our governments have very likely been interfacing with ET intelligences (or certainly have been aware of their existence) for some decades. In the widest sense, many of the proposals in this book are what can make our society a willing and capable partner to ethical ET civilizations as they reveal themselves on a mass scale, likely within this century, perhaps sooner than we think. While we may not all personally live to see the day we interact peaceably with our planetary neighbors, perhaps our children will.

The bottom line is that we 99% need to stand up and be counted and take back control of the situation on this planet. At its heart, the Occupy Movement is about that. I have personally been inspired by how the Occupy Movement has evolved and taken traction. Let's hope it continues. Some of the ideas expressed in this book are very similar to those in the "unofficial" list of demands at one time posted on the Occupy website. Many of these ideas are keying off from known data, known issues, and known analysis by the most credible of sources. However, I sincerely doubt you'll find them explored in one volume, and as in depth, as they are here.

Before diving into the essays, you may have a couple of questions. First, why (outside of the fact that the final essay has that title) use the title "A World Without War?" Second, who am I to suggest such a thing? When I first searched the term "A World Without War" in 2006 (after writing the essay), there were a couple of references that stood out: Noam Chomsky's talk of that title delivered at the II

World Social Forum 2002, and Ruth Rosen's article posted in *Common Dreams*, originally published in the *San Francisco Chronicle* in 2002. Other than that, there were not many references to the term "A World Without War."

Later, particularly after the late Mario Rodriquez Cobos' "World March for Peace and Non-Violence" in 2009, a search on the term "World Without War" returned many more hits. So support for the idea (or at least its Internet presence) has grown exponentially since Chomsky and others introduced it, and a war-weary world seems a lot more interested in the topic.

My point is twofold: first, it is an idea whose time has come. Second, the term is a metaphor, like Reagan's "City on a Hill," for a better world. In terms of this book, "A World Without War" expresses an intention of my own that leads me to the second question posed above: Who am I to suggest it? This is precisely the question that those in power want you to ask, and perhaps even react negatively to, because most in power would prefer us not to ask big questions. Because if you and I together, *en masse*, do start asking these questions, the probability of our current (dysfunctional) system remaining in place is highly unlikely, and the likelihood of solutions are quite high. Because, as a believer in humanity, I feel that once the people are awake to their own potential, solutions for a variety of social ills are not far behind.

To quote from Chomsky's talk on "A World Without War" from 2002—he stated it well:

> What remains of democracy is to be construed as the right to choose among commodities. Business leaders have long explained the need to impose on the population a 'philosophy of futility' and 'lack of purpose in life,' to 'concentrate human attention on the more superficial things that comprise much of fashionable consumption.' Deluged by such propaganda from infancy, people may then accept their meaningless and subordinate lives and forget ridiculous ideas about managing their own affairs. They may abandon their fate to the wizards, and in the political realm, to the self-described 'intelligent minorities'

who serve and administer power.

To sum up, I suggest we all begin overcoming any sense of futility and take our power back, realizing that many more of us need to grapple with the big questions of life, and then to come together in common cause and mutual respect to find solutions.

A lot of you reading might say this is all impossible. I'm more of an optimist. And while some will say it will take decades for many of the ideas in this book to come about, events in the short-term may indeed hasten that debate. But they likely will come about, or we will not evolve into a society that resembles anything that we call human. To define "being human" in a positive light, to forge a future in which such a thing known as a human being is a good and beneficial thing, and not something to be ashamed of or to lower our heads about—these are the challenges we face. And we are up for the task.

Don Thompson
January, 2012

Author Note: The essays in this book have been lightly edited, at times for content. In general, they reflect the essays as first published online. Most of the original essays still exist online should one like to compare the online and published versions. While no notes are included in this edition, major references are noted in the text and can be easily searched on the Internet.

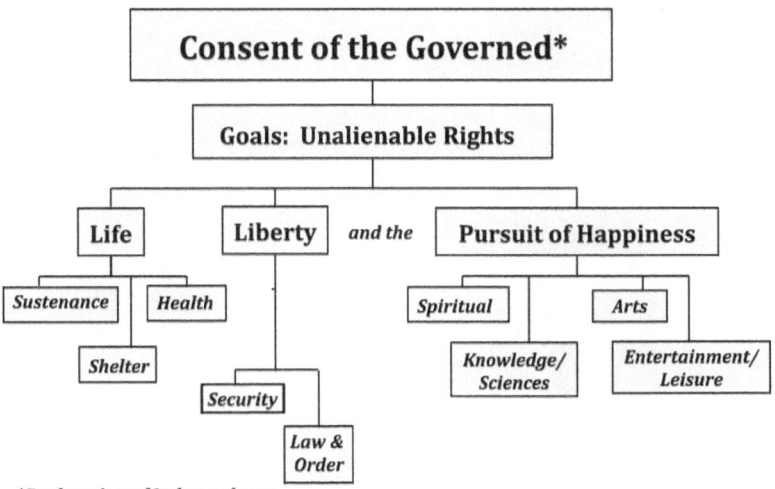

THE FOUNDATIONAL FRAMEWORK

Source: Joint Planning & Development Office: Challenges in Evaluating Advanced Technologies, Yuri Gawdiak, NASA/JPDO

THE NEW MEDIA AGE

(2000)

"[As for the Arab Spring, 2011] it is fair to say that, on the whole, the Arab media were largely muzzled and acted mainly as mouthpieces for their governments… But it was this weakness and lack of credibility which led the region's young to turn to the unrestricted and democratic world of digital media. Here they discovered not just the freedom to speak their minds without fear but also the power of solidarity and networking. Frustrations were shared, ideas discussed, slogans agreed and solutions hammered out. The result was the springboard for a democratic revolution." —Nabil Al Sharif, former Media State Minister, Jordan

Every television a network. Everyone a director. Desktop films, Guerrilla filmmakers, and democratized distribution. User-driven programming. The Fall of the Media Elites.

We've got a New Media Age on our hands.

It's a revolution of sorts. The top down, dictatorial relationship between media providers and their passive audience is ending. Enter media democracy.

What does it mean? Where will it go? Who will survive?

This paper addresses some of these questions. The goal is to provide a framework from which we can navigate. Or at least another perspective that, when colliding with one's own personal paradigm, creates some kind of shift or "ah hah."

Or maybe skepticism and "give me a break." Read on and hopefully you'll be swayed.

DEFINING THE AGE

What characterizes the New Media Age? The following table looks at some of the differences between the old and new media ages.

OLD MEDIA AGE	NEW MEDIA AGE
Top down programming	Bottom up programming
Genre-driven	Niche-driven
Homogeneous	Fragmented
Centralized	Decentralized
National	Regional/Community
Analog	Digital
Genres differentiate programming	Creativity and quality differentiates programming
Push	Pull
Channel surf	Multi-screen viewing
Broadcast/Cable	Broadband
Passive	Active/Interactive
Dumbed down	Avante-garde
Censored	Uncensored
High and low budgets	Micro budgets
Independent filmmaking	Guerrilla filmmaking
Incremental/Slow	Revolutionary/Fast
Desperate	Courageous
Promotes products	Promotes non-products

Some of the above that's listed under the "New Age" is really already happening in the "Old Age." So the characterizations blur. But the distinctions in a broad sense hold water when you look at what is essentially a movement away from the old age and toward the new age that has been happening for several years and now accelerated by the Internet.

HOW TO COMPETE

How does one compete in such an environment? In my view, the only way to compete is to go with it. To become it. To in fact help it. The way not to compete is to fight it. Because it is happening, will happen, and will not stop. The Movement is a force unto itself.

The Movement is driven by technology, but also by people seeking alternatives. The System has upset a lot of people. Voices have been silenced. Creativity squelched. The Least Common Denominator has been forced down everyone's throats. Many feel victim to media pollution and being dumbed down to the point of numbness.

As for the so-called alternatives, many have co-opted the bohemian style but not the content. Many artists today look like Bob Dylan but feel like Bob Dole.

WHAT THE PEOPLE WANT

The conventional wisdom is that content providers today are responding to what people want. And because the economics of media production are expensive, they are forced to provide to the majority.

Mediocrity in the media has become a habit, something run by apathetic and cynical producers who don't believe in anything but the bottom line.

But who is the "majority" that most producer's cater to? The "majority" is really human nature. The majority as it applies to programming and content is appealing to the most basic human impulses because we know that works to get an audience. We also know it keeps us in an unending cycle of sameness.

High production costs have forced programmers to appeal to the many. Now those costs can come down. Digital video cameras are cheap and ubiquitous. A non-linear editing solution can be purchased for under $10K that used to cost hundreds of thousands of dollars. Internet content distribution is cheap and universal, and with broadband will have the same quality as broadcast or cable television. The result is that producers are empowered by a new economic dynamic that allows them to produce much more cheaply and allows them to appeal to a much narrower demographic, even narrower than the current fragmented media market.

Lowered production costs and niche programming force content providers to appeal to the few, and the few will soon be much more localized than you think.

A cottage industry is arising of "desktop filmmaking" and "video publishing." Many homes will become production facilities. Many other New Media Age storefronts will also arise. The New Media Age production facility will become as ubiquitous as Kinko's. The new communication paradigm will shift from the written word and PowerPoints to the edited image and PowerVideos.

We will both lose language and find it anew. The use of images to communicate will be almost as ubiquitous as text. DV mail will be as common as email or voicemail. And that's just the start.

MARKET DRIVERS

Some of the market drivers for the New Media Age include:
— Revolutionary Change
— Values
— Non-Products
Let's look at each in detail.

REVOLUTIONARY CHANGE

We are in a decade of revolution. This revolution is occurring on many fronts, and has both positive and negative ramifications.

The technology revolution will continue. Broadband and Internet media distribution will offer a broader access mechanism for voices that have rarely, if ever, been heard. And no one will filter this media from on high. Individuals will instead make their own decisions as to what to watch, and when.

A social revolution is also brewing. Issues related to the environment, global economics and education will continue to become more and more important as the decade progresses. These voices will demand a vehicle for expression. The Internet, broadband and low–cost digital content creation technologies will provide that vehicle.

On the mainstream media front, the irony is that the lowered cost of production enables media providers to lead an audience, if they so choose. The reason is that the New Age Media economics promote creativity in such a way that will not only enable new voices to be heard but demand it. Newness and change will be such a hot commodity that the market itself will demand revolutionary change.

Because the niche-oriented nature of broadband will take more and more mindshare from traditional audiences, traditional media will be forced to embrace a more diverse and fragmented programming agenda. The concept of a mass audience will in some ways disappear.

Revolutionary change will in fact drive the economy. The New Media Age is the voice of that change.

VALUES

Initially, we may see a lot of programming crap as a result of the "revolution" (mostly because of people trying to do Hollywood on the Cheap). But we will also view the new, the truly revolutionary, the enlightening. We'll see that much of New Media Age will be driven by values.

The least common denominator will give way to the greatest individual potential, The Age of Media Enlightenment. Value-oriented. Altruistic. Not altruistic so much by choice, but inevitable altruism by the laws of evolutionary change.

Values will propel the New Media Age because a large section of the market will demand values to counter the numbing downward spiral of media content that the cynics see as inevitable.

Values don't necessarily imply uniformity of opinion. New coalitions will form that might seem strange bedfellows at first. Many former enemies may unite against the value-less media in order to counter a general trend toward programming that emphasizes the darker side of human nature.

The vehicle for distributing this new media content will be new broadband networks accessed by Internet portals. The portals, which will be owned and operated by a few large companies, will nonetheless have open access to thousands of New Media Age content providers. This open access, when combined with interfaces that allow people to create their own programming, will mean that there will be absolutely no commonality in the interface to the media. People will define their own interfaces, in effect, their own networks. Even though the portals will be under the banner of the Old Guard media, open access will allow people to create their own media world, and many will do so.

They will do so because the current media meets the needs of the corporations they serve and not the people. Over decades, corporate interests have conditioned people's expectations and tastes, greatly influencing the so-called "market." This will change in the New Media Age, where people will define the nature and scope of their media experiences. Conventional wisdom will no longer apply. That status quo will be shattered in a way no one can quite foresee.

NON-PRODUCTS

Non-Products began with shareware and "free stuff." Advertising itself is a form of Non-Product. The idea is that a free commodity or experience will help to sell a paid for commodity or experience. A free product is a non-product. Values, truth and ethics are also non-products.

More and more, people are demanding that what was once charged for become free. The free music movement is a prime example. In the future, films will follow suit. This trend will only accelerate no matter what Jack Valenti wants.

Eventually, copyright owners may need to give up the idea that they can somehow control the sharing of content and will have to look to other ways to generate revenue from their products. Business models that don't depend on copyright must and will flourish. The Old Guard will be able to create stopgaps to the trend, but ultimately it will not be possible to forestall. The media industry will have to accept that the model of property rights as applied to physical property does not neatly apply to digital media, which can be replicated *ad infinitum* cheaply and universally.

Moreover, free sharing might not be such a bad thing. In the case of music, the free sharing of an individual song may lead to the sale of a CD the song is associated with. Thus the individual song becomes a non-product to sell the CD.

With films, trailers can serve the same purpose. During a certain early release window, a film's trailer can be distributed for sharing on the Internet, which will lead to the sale of the film's theatrical release or video/DVD (this is in fact already happening with some films). Thus the trailer becomes a non-product on the Internet, an entertainment in its own right that is a tie-in to a product.

Non-Products will rule. But for traditional Old Guard companies to survive, they will need to tie non-products to products. For the new guard media, low costs and embedded product placement will enable them to compete and survive.

CONCLUSIONS

The New Media Age is both exciting and intimidating. There are social and economic reasons for the shift from the old to the new, with the Old Guard representing certain values that will be questioned and challenged.

Hollywood will certainly survive, as it has survived in the past with the advent of television, cable, and other innovations. The theatrical experience will certainly be maintained as part of the Hollywood system. Post theatrical release, the Internet will become a major method of distributing and change the dynamic completely.

The post theatrical market for film content will so change with the Internet that Hollywood will have to adopt hybrid business models that incorporate elements of television sponsorship, guerrilla filmmaking, and content subscription. They will inevitably have to open up their content libraries fully to the Internet, because if they don't, they will find their content being shared freely no matter what stopgaps are put in place. At least if they open up their libraries they can use advertising embedded in their content (either as a trailer or ad, or product placement), and offer subscriptions or syndication.

While the art of prediction is certainly a precarious one, some of these trends may well come to fruition and are in fact well on their way to becoming reality. With that in mind, we believe that the future can be shaped in a positive way. Toward this goal we dedicate our work.

IS BIG MEDIA THE ANTI-CHRIST?

(2003)

"The lies the government and media tell are amplifications of the lies we tell ourselves. To stop being conned, stop conning yourself." —James Wolcott

If you haven't been following the evolution of Internet activism, then you're missing probably one of the most significant trends of the last few years. Case in point is the campaign to stop media consolidation as reflected in a new set of FCC rule changes allowing for a new round of media mergers. These changes were opposed by a broad swath of the American public from all sides of the political spectrum. MoveOn.org garnered no less than 180,000 online letters in protest against the rule changes in an attempt (at least) to have them postponed until Congress could do a little bit more chin-wagging over the subject. After MoveOn's Internet blitz, supplemented by newspaper ads featuring Rupert Murdoch as a kind of poster child of Evil Media, no less than Trent Lott himself stood up and bemoaned the changes and—along with democratic colleagues in a rare show of bi-partisanship—complained how FCC chairman, Michael Powell, had broken tradition, ignoring a Congressional request to shelve the rule changes until further inquiries could be made. Instead, Powell went ahead and barreled forward anyway, like Bush into Iraq.

While MoveOn cannot be credited solely for the public's reaction against the FCC, I do believe the Internet onslaught was key to moving opinion among leaders, and giving them the courage to stand up where they might have otherwise nodded off. The ability to quickly (literally within a day or two) harness such a broad and resounding voice of protest is perhaps unparalleled in history. It is one of the bright spots in our otherwise downward spiral toward media mediocrity, uniformity, groupthink and profit myopia. The Internet, if considered to be part of the media, is probably the only true outlet for alternative sources. One wonders how long it will last.

In an interview for *SolPix*, I asked Todd Gitlin if he thought that media types thought strategically about the *why* of their approach and worldview—if media was created with a specific agenda in mind. My question hinted at the "C" word, conspiracy—often a code word with mainstream news interviewers for "insane, paranoid and crazy" when guests such as Gore Vidal question nasty things like the root-causes of September 11 and Waco. It seems that the right-wing is in cahoots with stupid, shallow, lazy reportage and has conspired to give us damn little *why* in the recent past. To get back to Gitlin, he believed that at least from the corporate side, no conspiracy existed—all was based on profit. In other words, news editors were not saying "Don't explore the why" because they got the word from on high. It's just that they felt exploring the why would cause them to lose money, or they were self-censoring based on conventional wisdom.

So to follow Gitlin's thinking, MSNBC, in hiring conservative commentator Michael Savage and dropping the liberal Phil Donahue, was responding to ratings and profit, not to ideology. There was no grand strategy to move MSNBC to the right in order to become "Fox light." Decisions on programming are supposedly dispassionate, existing in a vacuum, based on some grand calculation of return on investment. With all due respect to Todd Gitlin, I have to believe that the notion that media executives operate in some kind of objective market purity doesn't jive with reality. Media executives are paid to sniff trends and react, and to react in a fashion that will increase profits, to be sure. Yet the fact that they are so "flexible" in their movement to dump Donahue and take on Savage belies the true problem, that is, the inevitable corruption of a system based solely on money and not balanced by basic humanity—a form of corruption that exists no matter what the media's ideological face.

The fact is that the "givens" of modern capitalism crucify anyone who questions its validity. Modern notions of capitalism and consumerism are so above reproach as the binding "good" of society that to question them is like questioning the veracity of the Pope. Truth be told, the cold, hard decisions of the boardroom are often self-fulfilling prophesies generated within a world of market "givens" that can be controlled, if desired, by the marketers themselves. MSNBC may have been reacting, but it was reacting with a strategic change of course in mind. This overall course is laid out quite clearly by the élites of global capitalism, and it has little to do with democracy and the promotion of the general welfare.

MSNBC's decision to go with Savage was not unlike all those good capitalists in Nazi Germany supporting Hitler because it was easier, it was convenient, and it lined their pocketbooks if they happened to be war contractors or in an industry that would profit from the war. The truth is that to be "on board" with the current trend toward corporate globalism and groupthink is a prerequisite for survival in the boardrooms of any corporation, be it media or otherwise. As always, the ultimate issues come down to fear and control, and yes, money. But money within a context of a system that knows it must perpetuate itself and not promote ideas that would destroy its hold on the populace—even if those ideas would promote the ideals this country was founded on. The result is "the system"—an alliance of business and a quasi-democracy that exists in its shadow. As Ned Beatty so aptly revealed to Howard Beal in the film *Network*—"The world, Mr. Beal, is a business."

The system has a contract with the people—it takes care of you, it feeds you and it houses you, and in the United States it pays you better than the average starving Asian day laborer because you can vote and often they can't. In return, either you let it alone or you support it. And as long as the contract is met we don't mind if our media has a kind of numbing sameness to it, that one commentator can be swapped in for another, that none of them can think beyond their earpiece—much like William Hurt's character in the poignant and prophetic *Broadcast News*. News and media are foremost and primarily entertainment, fodder and fill-in to keep us distracted long enough until the really important message—the advertisements—kick in. And we don't mind, because we're fed and we're housed by the Holy Mother System—for the most part at least. And we believe the myths and fantasies created by the media organizations that placate us, make us feel like we're good and moral, when in reality we are in many ways rotting, and both ourselves and our media masters are cowards to the core. And even if we don't know it consciously, we feel the numbing psychological pain of it, and take increasing amounts of anti-depressants and fixate on numerous addictions in order to avoid confronting our own awareness. And of those addictions, the addiction to self-aggrandizement is paramount—the perennial re-enforcement of the myth that Americans are special, endowed with manifest destiny, and can forever depend on God's special status to keep us out of harm's way. And the purveyor of that myth is largely the media.

Now what is "the system" and what is so bad about it? It's not unlike *The Matrix*, where the character of Cypher—the betrayer of Neo and Morpheus—looks into the hollow eyes of Agent Smith and tells him how he prefers the illusion of the Matrix to the reality of the world. Was Cypher wrong? I must say that he may be right, but to deal with the reality of our world is different from dealing with the reality in *The Matrix* in that the reality of our Matrix—a largely impoverished and/or exploited third world living in a perpetual state of suffering tantamount to our Great Depression or worse, kept that way in many instances through the support or institutions and injustices that we have a complete and utter ability to influence, but don't—the truth is that the reality of that world will eventually come shattering down with problems that no movie star or super hero (or even president) can stop with a quick karate kick or gun.

How will this occur? In one of two ways: sudden chaos or slow death. Certainly, slow death is the preferred method, as it enables the system to make even more money in its attempt to cure the diseases that it propagates as a result of its value system. Let me give an example. I recently visited a tourist attraction/outlet store just outside of Gettysburg, PA. Inside the huge, Felliniesque building sitting in the middle of a rural landscape was a fantasy land of American crafts: wooden ducks, teddy bears, and a plethora of other handicrafts—and all capped off with an elaborate, museum-like overview of the company's founders and history. The owner had begun humbly in Vermont, where he and his wife had made little wooden decoy ducks by hand. Now the company was NYSE listed, shown regularly on QVC, and billed as the "most humongous teddy bear store in the world." And it was. Inside were hundreds of people, mostly crammed in on bus tours, wandering aimlessly and buying the cute little critters, and almost all of those people were quintessentially fat, as is the American norm.

And each of these little bear things and "American" craft items were made, in many instances, in China (at least, based on my admittedly unscientific sampling—but you get the point). And these overweight, anxious and numbed consumers, all force-fed like some kind of *foie gras* goose, stumbled around in a kind of paxil fog, queuing up to buy these little bears they probably thought were made in the Good 'Ol USA by little handimakers in rural wherever. And what they were sold was what, primarily? The myth of themselves, the innocence of that myth, manipulated, packaged, and foisted back on them when the exploitive economic reality underlying it was completely different, even contradictory to, the myth itself. And this is exactly what news commentators did recently with the war against Iraq. They fed our own myth back to us, force-fed us to the point where we could only capitulate, overpowered by the force of their arguments and their assumptions as they rolled over the war's contradictions and unanswered justifications, like so many Humvees through the desert.

Are there weapons of mass destruction? Are there conflicts of interest with the Bush and Cheney *vis-a-vis* war contractors? Were lies told? Who cares? Just move on, because the consumer is so numbed by the process that he'll just move on to the next item in the queue, whether that's a war or a teddy bear, ever willing to serve his country by becoming increasingly depressed and diabetic. But all the better for pharmaceuticals who dominate the airwaves with their commercials anyway. But this moving on, unlike that promoted by MoveOn.org, takes us away from our inevitable confrontation with reality. This moving on takes us toward the grave, both spiritually and physically.

From Associated Press, June 15, 2003, regarding American Troops raid in FALLUJAH, Iraq: "To diffuse animosity [among the populace], the troops followed up their assault by delivering humanitarian supplies, including school books, medicine and even teddy bears."

CARTOON NATION

(2004)

"Ninety-eight percent of American homes have TV sets, which means the people in the other 2% have to generate their own sex and violence."
—Franklin P. Jones

I ventured into a video store the other evening and rented *Under the Tuscan Sun* (director Audrey Wells). This bold act was prompted by my significant other, who had a hankering for a little Italian landscape. I told her that I heard the movie was supposed to be bad; I wasn't quite sure where I had heard that, but I had read it somewhere. Probably the *Washington Post*—Stephen Hunter or somebody. Or maybe A.O. Scott of the *New York Times*. At any rate, I suggested we rent *Pirates of the Caribbean*, since I wanted to see why Johnny Depp's performance had gotten so much attention. I asked the manager of the store what she thought. She definitely advised we should pass on *Tuscan Sun* and go for *Pirates*. She went on to say that Depp had based his performance on Keith Richards (the rock band, the Rolling Stones' Keith Richards, I assumed), and I joked: "I hope he doesn't look as wrinkled as Keith Richards." Neither the manager (probably in her 40s), nor the cashier (probably in hear late teens or early 20s) laughed at the joke. I wound up renting both movies.

Back at home, instinct told me to put on *Tuscan Sun*. Maybe it's my rebellious nature. I live in a kind of suburban *la la* land, not quite what I'm used to, since I just spent a lengthy stint in downtown New York, wearing black and going to a lot of art house films. Now I go to a Cineplex and the closest thing to an art film in the area we're likely to see is *LadyKillers*—which I'd really call a kind of art house cartoon. But more on that later.

At any rate, *Tuscan Sun* wound up being one of the sweetest films I've seen in a long time. And its sheer sweetness prompted me to ponder: what the hell was it about this sweet little film that made the manager at the video store frown like as if to watch it would be painful, much too painful for me to bear, and that we should opt instead for Johnny Depp? What are people trying to protect me from? Terrorists? Anarchy? Or is it something much simpler: pain?

Pain. That's what *Tuscan Sun* was about, in a nutshell. Pain and how someone deals with it. It was a somewhat serious, somewhat human, somewhat get under your skin kind of film that you can (if you've gone through a very painful experience) relate to. *Tuscan Sun* was about pain and how one woman learns from it. The performances were simple and direct. Diane Lane was quirky and charming and a lot of fun to watch.

Anyway, this series of events led me to some pondering, and a subsequent conclusion about U.S. culture I thought worthy to share with *SolPix* readers. Many of us, certainly in the U.S., are becoming divided (or at least that's what they want us to believe) into Blue and Red state "types." We are also becoming divided into human beings and something else. I'm not sure what that something else is, but it doesn't seem to be human, because it isn't interested in stories that relate to anything resembling human beings. The stories this new breed or species like have to do with super things that can leap over buildings and devastate entire towns in video games. This new species seems to like destruction—the more of it the better—and revels in "squashing" the bugs, even if those bugs happen to be other human beings (such as in Iraq).

What this new species doesn't like is pain. That is, pain that they could possibly suffer. They do, however, like the (cartoonish) physical pain of others, inflicted with relish via digital effects, a kind of "gotcha" pain that says "I hurt you first." They like pre-emptive pain, such as inflicted on Iraqi war prisoners. This same spirit also shows up in films. Whether that be in commercial movies like *Pirates* or "art" films like *LadyKillers* and *Kill Bill* or "spiritual" films like *The Passion of the Christ*. Give me that pre-emptive, Looney-Tunes pain. It's appropriate for kids, little kids that can be easily led around by the nose by aggressive, confident politicians, defense secretaries and media parents—sorry, I mean *pundits*. Yeah, that kind of pain.

The pain of a Cartoon Nation.

Not real, personal pain—emotional pain, adult, human pain. That's considered *wimpy* pain. That kind of pain must be buffed out, censored, eliminated, digitally enhanced, and/or relegated like the coffins from Iraq to the "inappropriate." Emotional pain is what sex used to be (i.e., swept under the carpet), while nowadays painless, commitment-less, aggressive sex is all over the media, like Cheerios and Wheaties once were. I sound nostalgic, don't I? Or maybe reactionary, conservative? But am I, or do I just long for a basic humanity in our daily discourse, a humanity that often seems drowned out as the next newscaster cheerfully announces another 10 war dead in Iraq, followed quickly by images of Spring Break revelers in South Beach getting it on in bathrooms? And it was a good thing too, because I wasn't sure what values we're defending.

In America we have become parodies of the commodities we consume. We are so categorized, polled, discussed, pandered to, at once homogenized and demographically sliced and diced that we actually think of ourselves as products rather than humans. We are "Red" and "Blue" state people that are pro this or anti that. We are the fiction of Reality TV, where people are so out of touch with their own emotions that all they can feel is the artificiality of a performance reality that they somehow believe is more real than direct emotions garnered from unmediated (innocent?) experience. We are the numbingly same teenage accent and slang spoken by adults and kids alike. We are the college students who march to the "rebelliousness" of Spring Break with conformity not seem since Hitler Youth. We are the blockbuster sequels that deal in re-tread themes based on re-tread characters and types that are themselves based on a distorted facsimiles of reality once or twice removed from the original. And film reviewers speak of these contrivances as if they somehow contribute to culture in a positive way. And we all march in lockstep to the sham, munching on the popcorn and hoping our next distraction will not remind us of anything hinting at truth.

Like a cartoon, we have our own internal logic, reality be damned.

Boy, that sounded good! Considering the fact that I'll probably rent *Pirates of the Caribbean* next weekend, I better watch myself. Truth may be there too. Embedded, maybe, like a journalist in Iraq.

Yeah, blockbuster films. Many film reviewers, understanding they don't write to a human audience anymore, don't think about these films in terms of their impact on society, but instead how the particular star will use that film in a particular way to forward their career in a particular fashion. These films are seen in the context of an overall marketing or demographic plan, a plan that at its heart has the overarching morality of our nation: to make money, lots of it, and the quicker the better. I mean, there is urgency to cashing out, since Jesus is coming soon. Or is it the terrorists? Either way, I feel manipulated into believing it. Anyway, back to the point. Reviewers in general support blockbuster films because, after all, there's *so much goddamn money at stake.*

Money. Our core value. What we fight for. That's of course why we need to see the coffins of the Americans killed in Iraq (which are themselves emblems of our Cartoon Nation, sanitized and neat, like rows of Post-it notes on a computer screen). Leave it to America. When we deal with soldier consumption—sorry, *death*—we will be organized. However, having just lost my father, I know that the grief of those who lost family in the war is not so much organized as it is chaotic. Grief comes over you in waves and is indiscriminate, like a carpet bomb. It seems to take a life of its own, until it is done with you, leaves you a spent husk, and moves on to the next in line.

Back to the "Reds" and the "Blues." The *Washington Post* recently profiled a "Red State" person in a very in-depth article. In one telling section, this man read the Melitta coffee filter packaging as he prepared his morning brew, and noted that the company "plants four trees for everyone that it cuts down for its products." This Red State guy said: "What do I care?" Exactly.

The new species, be they a Rush Limbaugh Red or an Al Franken Blue, does not care because they don't want to hassle the messiness of feeling. They want to go through a series of actions, predefined by others, a Kodak Moment, mapped out kind of life that makes it easy. And this just doesn't apply to America. The new species is in fact globalized, whether they be Blue, Red, American, Christian, Arab, Jew, college kid or teenager—they seem to tend toward a simplistic, commodified, fundamentalist attitude that life comes down to the squasher and the squashee, and better to be the squasher then the squashed. The problem is that all this pain avoidance or rapid lashing out to get the other guy first won't ever lead to something that is required for global evolution: maturity. A maturity garnered through life experience and seen in films like *Tuscan Sun* that evoke a little-known emotion seen today: empathy.

It is a maturity, an empathy, apparently found more often on Melitta coffee filter packages than in government policies. In other words, maybe we should educate four (or maybe 4 million) poor children for each one killed by war. Why? Because we *empathize* with their plight. And maybe "I don't care" isn't the best response. But no… we only really care about our little neighborhoods, our little SugarLand Texas (the subject of the recent *Washington Post* article about the "Red" state that I mentioned), our neat little houses that look just like those neat little flags on those neat little coffins coming from Iraq.

By the way, a recent study stated that for the cost of maintaining our soldiers one month in Iraq, we could provide minimal education to all of the children in the developing world (U.S. $5 billion). But then, aren't we generous enough? After all, the U.S. gave a whopping $100 thousand to North Korea for its recent train catastrophe—that's about what Donald Rumsfeld spends on one plane ride to Iraq, I'm sure.

But back to *Tuscan Sun*. The humor evident in *Tuscan Sun* was much like my dry, pretty silly joke relayed in the video store, which told me why that manager and cashier didn't laugh when I told it, as if we all lived in parallel realities, and mine wasn't in sync with theirs. It was a kind of humor reminiscent of two other human-laced, woman-directed films: Sophia Coppola's *Lost In Translation* and Nancy Meyer's *Something's Gotta Give*. So maybe I'm becoming a little too "feminine" in my humor. A little too wimpy. Maybe I'm starting to sound like a Woody Allen movie, whose sense of humor is a little dated, a little too adult, for most under 40. Since I am over 40, I guess that explains it. I'm just trying to stay human, but might be waging a losing battle to the adolescents, be they in gross out comedies or the White House. We'll have to see. They may make a cartoon out of me yet. Until then, I feel like I'm Bill Murray in Tokyo, not wanting to come back to the U.S. until the adults take over again.

LAND OF THE FREE, HOME OF THE WIMPS

(2004)

"He who stands for nothing will fall for anything." —Alexander Hamilton

This year's election has been one of the closest, longest and most polarized in memory. Pollsters have conducted numerous surveys and showed a decisively anti-Bush, angry and united Democratic Party squaring off against an equally supportive pro-Bush Republican base. More than ever, the election has been left to those who can't decide until the last minute. Voters on the political fence, voters who need to be told which dessert to choose—these people have our fate in their hands. More often than not, people are swayed by negative campaigning, the direction of the wind, or how "likeable" or "stiff" or "like them" a particular candidate is. In short, we have the ever- fickle, undecided voter.

I've often wondered what drives undecided voters. Not being one of them myself, having voted consistently for the same party my entire life, and unable to bring myself to vote for the opposition, I wonder what it is that allows people to migrate with the political climate. After all, what is it that they are undecided about? Whether a particular candidate makes them "comfortable" or not?

With the parties becoming more clearly distinctive in this election cycle than in the past, there should be enough clarity to allow the undecided camp finally to step up to the moral plate and make a commitment to some kind of cohesive political viewpoint. In short, maybe they can all stop being wimps.

If they don't, the country will remain hostage to the kind of political mediocrity only mass indecision can engender.

Now one can argue that Kerry himself is an "undecided," and I'm sure he'll be called a wimp. His congressional votes have wavered—first he votes for Iraq and then against appropriations. He supported NAFTA but now swaggers against it. His position is shifting based on both political calculus and a re-assessment of the territory. (Ironically, this may make him more appealing to undecided voters than Bush, as they can identify with Kerry.) So, like Kerry, are all undecideds simply shifting with the appropriateness of a given political season, helping to subtly nudge the nation this way or that? Maybe, maybe not. My sense is that there are different types of undecideds, and I'll get to that in a moment.

Being a consistent political voter used to be easier when the Big Parties actually stood for something consistent. Now they co-opt one another so often that the once Low Tax, Limited Government Republicans have become the Big Spend (if still not Big Tax), Big Government Republicans. Moreover, the formerly fiscally irresponsible Democrats have become the scions of budget restraint, particularly under Clinton. So the kind of classic Federalist/Democrat vs. Small Government/Republican debate is difficult to perceive—and the ghosts of Jefferson and Hamilton, ever arguing the issue of limited government versus Federal might and central authority, find themselves throwing up their arms in despair when neither party represents a purist stance. To be sure, undecided wimpdom is more easily understood in this context.

But the undecideds I have most problems with are not those who struggle over how two candidates may divide them on issues that they care about—let's say abortion and the economy—where a voter has to weigh in on which issue, and therefore which candidate, takes precedence. These people I understand. The undecideds I'm speaking of are those who treat candidates like socks, or sweaters, or breakfast at IHOP. In others words, consumer voters. When I hear one of these consumer voters, in justifying a vote, say something like "I just really like him…" it makes me want to crawl under my nearest copy of The Constitution.

I'm not saying these people shouldn't vote, I'm just saying they should think about what they're doing before they touch the screen or punch the chad. Maybe read an Op-Ed or two, maybe study a little history—in other words, get a little intellectual spine in their lives.

Luckily for us all, a very nasty little trend may prompt such people into thought, something much more powerful than anything I or anyone else might write in a political piece. That is globalization.

You see, globalization has finally come home to roost, and every profession but those related to Kinkos and Starbucks can be potentially outsourced to India, China and Thailand. Undecideds who used to be swayed by trenchant factors such as charisma and likeability are now thinking these might be trivial topics when compared to the monster of Globalization that seems to be eating American jobs (even white collar jobs) like popcorn. But wait…we're all supposed to join the investor class, right? Tell that to the unemployed textile workers in South Carolina who love John Edwards, who got his anti-NAFTA religion about six months ago.

Of course the progressives all fear that all this anti-globalization talk among the Democrats will fade if they win, and the Republicans, if they win, oh well! Progressives fear that the global market economy is still really off the table, and even under a Democrat the continual erosion of worker rights, healthcare, environmental standards and the like will continue under the unrelenting pressure of WTO, NAFTA, and the Chinafication of everything—and that this will last until again, like in the Great Depression, we have a true economic meltdown. And yet, strangely, even a *faux* and insincere debate along these lines may force a situation on us all that will allow progressives to recapture the moral high ground from the right.

The modern stripe of activist, populist presidents with a moralistic flair can trace their line back to Teddy Roosevelt, who after McKinley's assassination decided Americans wanted change of the Trust Busting kind. Roosevelt, like his cousin after him, became one of the principal forces behind the focused use of Federal power to address corporate abuse and market imbalances. But Teddy Roosevelt, while important, was a stopgap predecessor to the real deal, his cousin Franklin. My sense is that our newly populist Democrats are also a stopgap. I don't think much will change in terms of job outsourcing and market reforms and the least common denominator rule of everything from Wal Mart to Hollywood. But none of that matters in the short term, because the newly populist rhetoric is aimed squarely at the undecideds, who will wield their swing votes with a vengeance, and could likely put a Democrat in the White House. And more importantly, the debate will have shifted back to a center of gravity that doesn't so much pit moralistic save-heterosexual-marriage types against the mayor of San Francisco, but rather pits morally outraged save-heterosexual-marriage types against even more morally outraged anti-globalization types, many from Southern and swing states.

If all works out in a positive sense, this will all be the beginning of a shift in American attitudes that will force us back to a kind of basic humanism, where politics is not manipulated by media hyperbole but rather fueled by a desire for fundamental human decency and fairness; where politics is not based on hatred and divisiveness, but rather on a political humanism reflected in our history by the likes of Franklin Roosevelt and Lincoln. And this is what the consumer-oriented undecideds really need to chew on—whether to grow up and join the ranks of human beings, be they religious or otherwise, who make positive moral choices, or to continually look to the latest negative ad in order to make their voting decision. For ultimately, being human is about choices, about taking a stand for something that transcends things that shift with every political election cycle. And that holds true for either side of the political equation—for as we will see this election season, morality can finds its voice among both the issues of the right and the left. Because at the end of the day, we all have to look ourselves in the mirror, and making that decision to look at that face, really look. This is perhaps the toughest decision of all. Finally, we all have to decide what we think is right.

PEACE AS STYLE

(2004)

"Peace is not merely a distant goal that we seek, but a means by which we arrive at that goal." —Martin Luther King, Jr.

With the current war in Iraq, the time is ripe to talk about peace movies. Films about peace, with peace as their central theme, speak to us in times of war, reminding us of alternatives. Peace films speak out against the atrocities of war, to be sure, but sometimes within the context of an overarching violence that is their stylistic core. At other times peace is embodied in both the style and theme of a particular film. Whether or not stylistically violent or peaceful, these films drive home the issues of war and the nature of peace in a way that provokes us, prods us, changes us. Moreover, some films show us a peaceful style within the context of a violent story. These films, in their own way, comment on violence and the Hollywood style that often supports it.

If popular films have dealt with issues of peace, they have often done so within the context of war: Oliver Stone's *Platoon*, Francis Coppola's *Apocalypse Now* (both about Vietnam), and Carol Reed's *The Third Man* (the aftermath of WW II), being three prime examples. These films heighten or even satirize the reality of war in order to rail against it, or to critique the unrelenting tendency of war to dehumanize. However, both *Platoon* and *Apocalypse* are in a sense cop-outs in that they are addicted to the power of violence as a dramatic device, use it to the utmost, squeeze us emotionally and mentally through its unrelenting presence, but yet do so in a way that fundamentally reminds us that violence is dehumanizing. Unlike modern films that glamorize violence, these films use violence as a tool to explore the human face of war. When Kurtz (played by Marlon Brando) drops the decapitated man's head in the lap of Willard (played by Martin Sheen) at the end of *Apocalypse*, Willard is horrified to the core and shaken by the brutality of the act. Kurtz, who has gone beyond remorse to a pathological sense of numbness, has become both superman and subhuman simultaneously, having stepped outside the bounds of humanity. Kurtz becomes both the detached father-God of heaven, distributing justice without a care for the concerns of humanity, while at the same time becoming the sub-human, the demon, whose very nature is self-destructive. This Yin-Yang nature of war, and of its effect on the human psyche, has been at the heart of the post-modern critiques of the realities of war. In *Platoon*, Charlie Sheen's Taylor and Willem Dafoe's Grodin both struggle to maintain their humanity under very de-humanizing circumstances and stand in contrast against the Kurtz-like Barnes, played by Tom Berenger.

Coppola's version of Kurtz (derived from Conrad's *Heart of Darkness*) is not unlike the character of Harry Lime in *The Third Man*, another dark anti-hero who is very much a product of the system. Both *The Third Man* and *Apocalypse* dealt with their dark anti-heroes in the same way: they were killed off by "good" men who did not lose their moral bearings in the struggle. In *Apocalypse*, Martin Sheen as Willard played the role of "approved" executioner, mirroring Joseph Cotton's Holly Martins, who killed Orson Welles' Harry Lime in *The Third Man*. I'm quite sure Coppola was influenced by *The Third Man* in writing the end for *Apocalypse*. (Interestingly, Welles had written an un-produced script of Conrad's *Heart of Darkness* and was definitely attracted to the persona of Kurtz). In both cases, Harry Lime and Kurtz stepped over the bounds of conventional morality, but at the same time retained enough of their former selves to condone their own destruction by their respective antagonists, the "good men" or better, the "good American" represented by Willard and Holly Martins. That Brando's Kurtz reflects on a river in the United States, "filled with the smell of gardenias," that was Willard's home state is no accident—the heaven of America (and by inference the "goodness" of Willard) is contrasted to the hell of the river (and the "evil" of Kurtz) in Southeast Asia.

The tendency of the American consciousness to require a pathological warrior to execute its atrocities, and then to disavow that warrior and ultimately destroy him, is a ritual of sacrifice played out every day in the Iraq War. However, today's Holly Martins or Willards are not fictional but very real in the minds of documentarians like Michael Moore, who with his *Fahrenheit 9/11* is the foil to our dark heart as personified in the also very real Bush family. Moore would of course very much like to sacrifice Bush in the electoral sense, even if Bush did what ultimately a majority of Americans felt needed to be done—remove Saddam Hussein. In a sense Moore is trying to take the responsibility of the Kurtzes of the world back to their origins: the leaders that create them. Again, both *The Third Man* and *Apocalypse* have this theme as central to their narratives—both Kurtz and Harry Lime are as much a product of war, a necessity of war if you will, rather than evil *per se*.

In Michael Moore's landscape, the real evil lies at the top, where the Bushes are cast with a dark and de-humanizing influence. Their minions are in turn mini-Kurtzes, and in Moore's *Fahrenheit 9/11*, we see these de-humanized soldier's face to face, playing their heavy metal music, seeing the enemy as a video game, reigning with fear and terror down upon them with a devilish delight—much like Kilroy (played by Robert Duval) did in *Apocalypse Now*. The warrior is not motivated by the goodness of the cause, but rather by the adrenaline rush of the kill. This corporate warrior (and I don't pretend that all of our solders in Iraq have this attitude, but commenting specifically on some of the soldiers seen in Moore's film and also evidenced in the Abu Ghraib prison abuse) has an attitude different from warriors of the past (at least in the way they are romanticized). It is as if the empty core of the rationale for the war in Iraq, as well as that in Vietnam (our last quagmire), provokes an attitude among the soldiers that must either make them monsters or destroy them psychologically. There is a large amount of evidence that suggests the latter, reflected in the increasing amount of Veteran suicides, is happening at a rapid rate.

That *Fahrenheit 9/11*—our modern version of *Apocalypse Now*—has moved from a fictional narrative where pathological soldiers are sacrificed to keep the corporate and political sponsors safe, to a new landscape tracing war back to the leaders and directly challenging them is, in many ways, remarkable. Hard as it may be to believe to many on the left, it shows the resilience of an American society which may be beginning to look inside of itself to find the root causes of its obsession with war, violence and domination. Moreover, we as a society can now tolerate a gadfly like Moore without persecuting him. Rather than persecute him, he becomes a millionaire, much like peace-promoting rock stars became rich during Vietnam. If Bush wins re-election, it will be interesting to see what happens to the Michael Moores of our society, and if this tolerance will continue.

While American peace films about war make use of violence to weave their stories (violence is in fact their *raison d'être*) other filmmakers take a different route stylistically and thematically when dealing with peace. These films subvert both the idea of war and the idea of violent filmmaking as a requirement of the Hollywood studio method. At the core of this violent filmmaking is violent and quick, "kinetic" editing that moves the narrative forward in an unrelenting fashion and forces the viewer forward like a runaway train. This editing style, almost taken to the point of absurdity these days with MTV, advertising and hyper-violent movies, all of which make it difficult to reflect on an idea or image, and a lot easier to manipulate somebody to your point of view. It is an ideal style for advertising and for cable channels such as Fox.

Filmmakers interested in subverting this violent and manipulative style may even do so within the context of genre. Hitchcock is the best example of this, particular with films such as *Vertigo* or *Rope*, where languid tracking shots and/or the lack of editing as in *Rope*, protested against the violent style of Hollywood even as he

(Hitchcock) dealt with stories that primarily focused on mysteries and crime. Hitchcock was very much a stylistic subversive.

The master of anti-Hollywood style is Michelangelo Antonioni. Many of his earlier films, such as *L'Avventura*, would be impossible for modern audiences to sit through without squirming in anxious pain (they were difficult enough for audiences in the 1950s and '60s). Antonioni would spend minutes on the spinning of a fan or wind through the trees, such as in *Blow Up*. The heirs to Antonioni are numerous, not the least of which is Theo Angelopolous, with films such as *Ulysses' Gaze* (starring Harvey Keitel), or *Eternity and a Day* (winner of the Palme d'Or at Cannes).

My own experiment in peaceful narrative, *Clouds*, certainly had the influence of Antonioni. In many ways *Clouds* was an anti-Hollywood narrative both in terms of style and the "passive" nature of its male protagonist (as a result men sometimes felt uncomfortable with the film). In terms of big budget Hollywood films, the most remarkable stylistic homage to Antonioni was *Castaway*, whose (general) lack of musical score, long tracking shots of the natural landscape of Tom Hanks' island prison made me literally gasp that director Robert Zemeckis was able to pull it off. I think Zemeckis was able to do so because he recognized the longing many people have for nature, for nature directly expressed and unmediated and unedited, and that it is getting harder and harder for people to find the peace associated with a pure and unmediated experience of natural beauty. People certainly would not generally sit down in front of the Grand Canyon for two hours and watch its colors change: audiences will, however, pay 10 dollars to sit and watch Tom Hanks on a remote Island for two hours, if nothing else because it's Tom Hanks, and not the vagaries of their own mind, they have to deal with.

Films that promote a peaceful style do as much to force us to question our attitudes toward violence as do films that overtly deal with violence and war. Antonioni, not much in vogue today although his influence continues (again, *Castaway* being a good example), was the prime mover (along with Jean Luc Godard) and proponent of the anti-Hollywood style (though Godard for different reasons), whose films often dealt with issues of peace—both inner and outer.

Antonioni will in my mind remain the quintessential art film director who confounds audiences and delights cinephiles that love his bravado and courage to buck the easy out of a Hollywood style, which traces its roots back to D.W. Griffith and *The Great Train Robbery*.

Peace can be both a stylistic and a thematic force. Peace can be forwarded by the style, and subverted by the story, or *vice versa*. Perhaps one day we will again see films that are both about peace and embody a peaceful style. We don't see much of that today, for our addiction to Hollywood editing keeps us glued to films that stylistically give us little room to think and very little peace. It seems to me somebody probably likes it that way.

LIBERAL WARFARE STATE

(2005)

"When you can whip any man in the world, you never know peace."
—Muhammad Ali

George W. Bush's re-election has forced many on the left-leaning side of the fence to ponder seriously about what another four years of George Bush will do to the U.S. and the world. It seems to me the most troubling issue surrounding Mr. Bush's re-election is the vast lack of awareness among voters as to what's really at stake. The Republicans have become masters at finding the carrot/wedge issue (for this campaign that was gay marriage) that gets socially conservative voters to the polls, and once the candidate is in power it's a typical bait and switch: the right wing tackles its real objectives, such as dismantling Roosevelt's New Deal.

In many ways the conservative movement of recent history is a counterpoint to Roosevelt, with Reagan being the anti-Roosevelt, if you will. And if anything, Bush is the anti-Kennedy. I don't need to draw too many parallels between Joe Kennedy Senior and Prescott Bush's tribes to make the point. On the other hand, Kerry was in a sense the shadow Kennedy, the echo of Kennedy (with the initials JFK), as Edwards was the echo of Bobby Kennedy (remember, together they were "John/John"). These signs are not completely coincidence or trivial: the national mindset seeks the "brand" of a great leader—and in a consumer society brands are what political life is all about. Kerry was very much the Kennedy brand from Massachusetts, while Bush was the cowboy brand from Texas.

There is a cultural dialog between Massachusetts and Texas, as each reflects different poles of the American personality—different brands of political consumerism. Perhaps more than anything, these poles delineate different stands on the appropriate use of power. Does a leader use power within the context of a global community? Or has the Imperial Nation State the sovereign right to wield whatever influence is necessary to keep the peace, promote prosperity, and protect its interests? This debate runs deep into the psyche of the nation: or at least the Republicans would like us to think so, and not ponder too much about what their neo-con intellectuals are really up to.

When John Kennedy made his well-known speech at the American University, saying he sought no "Pax Americana" he was trying to nullify or at least counterbalance the Imperialistic tendencies of the conservative pole of the ruling élite—and some said he was even murdered (in Texas) for taking that stand. But soon enough that speech was forgotten, and Lyndon Johnson (a Texan) has us deep into Vietnam, establishing our peculiar kind of democratic morality, even if that country didn't necessarily want it. The Vietnamese believed then, as the many Iraqis do now (particularly the Sunnis), that the American brand of democracy (force-fed at gunpoint) is a ruse and a sham, and that the real reasons for these American "adventures" are economic and about expansion of the U.S. sphere of influence. But after Johnson, the Democrats turned face, became "weak" and embraced the left. So the Imperial élite had to turn to the Republicans for all its answers. The apex of this movement can be found in the neo-conservative tracts of The Project for the New American Century and other think tanks formed during the 1990s while Clinton was still in office.

Fundamentally, the neo-con Republicans, for all of their talk of family values, are the party of Social Darwinism and survival of the fittest—and that translates into the need to show force and not yield overwhelming military might.

From this view, struggle is the birthright of nations and men, and without it societies will atrophy and die. On the other side are the utopians, who actually believe there may be some final, stable societal model that more or less answers the question once and for all "what is good government?", that finally humanity can arrive at some kind of peaceful coexistence and overcome its desire to kill one another. Europe has in some ways become this model, although the EU is quickly dismantling many aspects of the social democratic utopia that found its expression in the liberal welfare states of the U.K. and continental Europe. Its counterpoint, a work in progress that we see today in the U.S., is the liberal "warfare" state. Let me explain.

Forty or so years ago, the "true" conservatives in the U.S. (whether Democrat or Republican), seeing the anti-war movement, civil rights movement, women's and environmental movements stripping them of their relevancy, felt cornered by a conspiracy. For many on the right, this was captured neatly in a fascinating little book called *None Dare Call It Conspiracy*. At the center of this conspiracy theory was the fear of One World Government under the United Nations, originally dreamt up as the League of Nations by a ranting humanist and academic named Woodrow Wilson. To respond to this conspiracy, conservatives came up with their own counter-conspiracy, replete with the own think tanks, media and other institutions necessary to counter the onslaught of the leftist utopians who had the ear of *The New York Times*, the American Civil Liberties Union, the Council on Foreign Relations (CFR) and so on. All of these organizations were (according to the conspiracy) in lockstep with European Bankers and the U.N., and leading us toward institutionalized international cooperation, an end to wars, promoting "sustainable" development—in short, all kinds of nasty stuff that conservatives think can lead people to a weak-kneed dependency on governments. To be sure, there is and was a dark (can you say colonialist?) side to all these "neo-liberal" organizations that today has many progressives re-thinking all this.

The "true" conservatives (today represented by the libertarians) were eventually co-opted by the neo-conservative movement that uses (as convenient) some libertarian rhetoric and ideas regarding the dismantling of government (mostly so they can fund a more robust military) but has at its heart the desire for a revitalized Anglo-Saxon empire centering on the U.S. and Britain (notably, along with Australia, countries that made up the Iraqi "coalition"). The agenda, laid out quite explicitly in neo-conservatives such as Niall Ferguson's *Colossus: The Price of America's Empire*—and critiqued extensively by people such as author Gore Vidal and Lewis Lapham of *Harper's*—is to gut the liberal welfare state, entrench the world in perpetual war, and to squeeze the middle class so that the only option for young men and women in some parts of the country is to join the military, where disenfranchised Blacks and Hispanics become war fodder—"the new Celts" (as in Roman times) for the American Imperial Force (no, I didn't make this up!). The name of the game is keeping sufficient fear in the populace, and through constant fear and perpetual war they—the neo-cons—can maintain power and hide their dirty little secret, the 800-pound gorilla in the room: that the white Anglo-Saxon race is in decline, it is not reproducing as it once was, and is in fact in serious retreat.

Ask any good demographer of the political landscape, and they will tell you that the current changes in population in terms of race and urban lifestyle will tend to favor the Democrats and socially progressive policies. This fact is multiplied many times when looking from a global perspective. While the current commentators on CNN and Fox may tell you about a "mandate" for the political conservatives, quite the opposite is true. Lacking a mandate, neo-conservatives must turn to fear as a mechanism of maintaining control. Lacking good ideas and/or the conscience of the nation or the lessons of history, the neo-cons must manipulate, gerrymander and con (no pun intended) their way into power. My greatest fear is that this has all led to a level of corruption we can't even ponder, even if we continue with our internal myths to the contrary, forever believing we are "the world's greatest democracy."

Ironically, the world's greatest democracy may not be the U.S., but the Ukraine, whose population seems to care enough about voter fraud to do something about it on the streets.

You may ask yourself, why would they (the neo-cons) want to do such things? Why would they want such a global scenario when it can obviously harm so many people? The core reason may lie at the center of the human question: do we function predominately on the basis of hatred and fear, or do we evolve to function primarily on the basis of compassion? The natural evolution of mankind, if such an evolution exists, must logically be toward tolerance, increased democracy, and compassionate social policies that assure stability and the common good. Eventually, this democracy should extend into the corporate boardroom. But this evolution is quite obviously a threat to our current economic masters and their consumer economies that rely so much on fear and desire as the *leitmotifs* of their existence; economies that promote a methodically engineered mental space that keeps people ignorant of their slavery to the élites as it offers fake "freedoms" (freedom of choice between goods and services instead of freedom of mind).

The neo-cons promote the welfare of the oligarchs and élites, believe in an almost Mafia-like adherence to family as the core organizing principle for people, and tend to favor a resurgence of small, entrenched, aristocratic-like pools of wealth and influence (hence the need to kill the Estate Tax). Why? Because they believe in these pools of influence and believe that they create a world more favorable to their interests. Theirs is an "us" vs. "them" mentality. And make no mistake about it—we are the "them." These trends are already well in place in this country today and have been for decades. The disparity in wealth in this country has become almost laughable. There are maybe a few hundred "influentials" who wield a majority of the world's economic decision making power. It's no wonder so many people today are taking anti-depressants. Isn't it interesting how in both the conspiracy theories of the left and right, the rich always seem to come out on top?

The end game of the Liberal Warfare State is the support of liberal free market policies (hence the "Liberal" part); the creation of economic spheres where labor is cheap, pliant and hopefully under a dictatorship (China); a continual low level war against terror; keeping the lowest level of the labor pool in this country in check and militarized (can you say video games?); an ever more "Romanized" and violent entertainment geared toward keeping the masses in an ignorant and cynical place; manipulating elections through a variety of techniques (some fraudulent); virtual control of the corporate news media (all owned by the "influentials"); enhancing the power of the police state; keeping society divided by values-based "wedge" issues; and allowing the Internet as a method for the disenfranchised intellectual to vent his or her spleen (I guess I'm one of those intellectuals). In the meantime, global trade agreements create a meta-state of corporate power where the influentials reside and run the show. If anyone recognized this New World Order of the Liberal Warfare State, it would be George Orwell. Or better, the CIA in Latin America in the 1980s (the "Petri dish" for a lot of this stuff). And guess who's going to be the new Intelligence Czar? A product of that 1980s CIA "Iran-Contra" Central America, John Negroponte (the former Ambassador to Honduras, 1981-85).

The only threat to the Liberal Warfare State is widespread knowledge of its existence and a desire to reveal and end it among an aware population that rallies to the cause. Aware and engaged people will always be the sole enemy of the entrenched status quo. So in this sense the new U.S. that landed on our doorstep on September 11, 2001 is an opportunity to continually unite progressives. If that happens, Mr. Bush and all of his colleagues, and their dreams of Imperial Glory, will not last that long, and we can get on with the business of human evolution. If not, we may well be in for a long, dark ride.

THE RULE OF CAPITAL

(2006)

"For capitalism, war and peace are business and nothing but business."
—Karl Liebknecht

According to Professor Daniel Robinson of Oxford University, there were more law books sold in Revolutionary America than in all of England combined at the time. Statesmen in British Parliament of the era in fact commented on how well read, erudite and versed in law the Americans tended to be. Young men like James Madison wrote and thought well beyond their age. John Adams, who along with Thomas Jefferson kept one of the largest libraries in all of the United States, scribbled notes in his dog-eared editions, conducting running arguments with his philosophical competition—often referred to as luddites and dunderheads—but nonetheless considered. To Adams, the only "axis of evil" was ignorance.

Cicero, Roman senator and favorite among the revolutionary American thinkers, spoke of two kinds of Roman law: *jus gentium* and *jus civili*, with the former being the "laws of nations applicable to all human beings" and the latter the "civic law or the specific laws of localities." For example, while the parking ticket regulation might differ in Rome and Athens (*jus civili*), both have laws against murder (*jus gentium*). *Jus gentium* was the precursor to the enlightenment notion of natural law and the natural rights of men, on which the Declaration of Independence and the Constitution were based.

The Founding Fathers believed in the rational human being, who, applying his or her reasoning, understood that certain things were right and wrong, that it was not good to steal or lie, to murder or mistreat others, and that such an understanding was in fact a requirement for entry into the body of human civilization. Moreover, it is the rule of law, as understood going back to Roman law—not the "laws of persons"—that should be the ultimate purveyor of justice in the human world. It is these precepts: the rule of law, the natural rights of human beings, the understanding that rational beings have as a very part of their nature an intrinsic understanding of right and wrong, and moreover certain rights—to life, liberty, happiness and (to some thinkers) property—that these rights are considered inalienable, part and parcel of our very nature and birthright as people.

In light of our current situation, we must consider these ideas and precepts. What is the current situation? I will cite two macro events of major impact on the current development of nations and individuals: globalization and the War on Terror. Both have seen extra-judicial strategies, formulated and carried out with certain exigencies in mind that are not necessarily in concert with the needs of common people and through which the rule of law can be usurped and replaced by something else. For lack of a better term, let's call it *the rule of capital*—because it is capital that takes precedence over people's natural rights and the concept of *jus gentium* within the new world order.

We have today herds of lawyers and administrators—perhaps some well-intentioned but certainly all well paid—populating large buildings in Washington DC, who seem to have lost sight of the ideals on which this country and in fact civilization itself was founded, and of the rule of law. They are busy formulating both trade laws and terror laws that allow for the carrot and stick of the rule of capital. The carrot is the promise of global prosperity, the stick is that the status quo order must be maintained in order for security to be upheld. The *leitmotif* of this situation has its roots in human nature itself; one could say that what is really working is as old as the ages—fear and desire.

In terms of the War on Terror, the thinking becomes quite simple: there are those human beings who have transgressed the rules of humanity and taken on the mantel of the subhuman when they became terrorists, and therefore we must respond with a subhuman response in order to confront these "enemy combatants." Such is war. The War on Terror.

The argument goes that this war justifies a subhuman response; we must react to the demons by using their own tactics; like Kurtz in *Heart of Darkness* we must become the darkness in order to control it. People like Vice President Cheney will note that any skirting of the "rule of law" while executing the War on Terror was in fact necessary to save the lives of scores of innocents. Whether or not he is right we can never know. What we can know is that his thinking runs counter to the thinking of the Founding Fathers. What the Wolf Blitzer on CNN cannot tell us, the lessons of history can. Dick Cheney would have appeared as a dangerous mind to many of this country's founders.

In terms of globalization, there is the supposed requirement for a meta-legal framework of capital that, through a series of international organizations such as the World Trade Organization (WTO), set up a meta-national and extra-judicial framework that perverts the notion of *jus gentium* and *jus civili*. This is because the trade laws of nations as reflected in the WTO and its agents quite plainly favor the rule of capital over the rule of law and of the natural rights of persons. Simply put, the result is that a few hundred people have become enriched beyond conception, while poverty in the United States is on the rise. According to the *Washington Post*, the world's richest 400 are now all billionaires.

One could argue that globalization has literally lifted millions out of poverty, particularly in Asia, and that this in itself proves my argument wrong. However, while free traders have long argued that human rights and freedoms would increase quite naturally from free trade and consumer freedoms, this has not proved to be the case. In fact, the faddish Chinese youth often seem quite happy with their ability to dye their hair blue and dance to rock music, regardless of the fact they can't vote. This reality is more a failure of moral leadership than of China's young people—we simply have come to value consumer freedom more than political freedom. If the Chinese and Americans share common human values, these certainly aren't related to human rights: any shared values have more to do with having fun and not thinking too much—particularly about politics and how one's rights are either non-existent or being slowly eroded. As a case in point, "extra-judicial" mechanisms are quite commonplace in the Chinese legal system: in corruption cases, forced detentions are quite the norm. This is a dangerous situation: with the War on Terror, we seem to be taking China's lead rather than providing an example. Ultimately these kinds of compromises in the rule of law will unravel. Our prosperity—a prosperity based at its core not on capital, but on human freedom, initiative and entrepreneurship.

Those arguing for the rule of capital state that it constitutes the free flow of trade and that capital is the precursor to human rights, that free trade must precede a free humanity. The fact is that quite the opposite is true. Even China, which one could say is the emblem of authoritarian capitalism on the rise, survives only on the back of freedom—namely that it is the freedom of the West where the prosperity developed that gives the Chinese exploitable primary markets.

According to the International Federation on Human Rights:

> Today, the WTO interprets the principles of international law in a limited fashion, even selecting certain principles according to its own interests and agenda. Under a pretext of wanting to "depoliticize" trade, the WTO tries to distance itself from obligations stemming from the primacy of international human rights law over other international treaties. Moreover, the actual functioning of the WTO gives priority to the wealthiest countries in a disproportionate manner, preventing entire regions from reaping the benefits of international trade.

The prosperity of the few and the War on Terror, which seems strangely to exist in its wake, are driven by the rule of capital. Tactics and techniques unthinkable within the framework of constitutional law become acceptable within this world view. Within this framework, the forced arrest of persons, without due cause, and their subsequent detention for months or years without trial, and the ability of the Government to basically torture these individuals without due process (all common practices after 9/11), become the norm of behavior in numerous detention facilities maintained by the CIA and the military in Eastern Europe and other locations. One very visible example is kept within the confines of Guantamo Bay, Cuba. This same kind of logic allows for the setting up of extra-judicial alternatives that allow corporations to usurp national laws (i.e., labor, human rights and environmental laws) and in essence function outside of any notion of *jus gentium* or *jus civili*. Again, the notion of *jus gentium* or "laws applicable to all nations" becomes skewed and corrupted by the exigencies of the powerful. And again in China, extra-legal actions and torture can be the norm for citizens. The question becomes, how quickly will we follow? Are we one nuclear suitcase bomb away from becoming like China?

Recently, the U.S. Supreme Court and U.S. Senators of both parties have seemed anxious to reel in the more egregious problems of the extra-legal War and Terror, and a compromise has been sought between hawks and doves on the issue. Still, apparently the limitations of torture will not be sufficiently controlled; political commentators have been quick to note that Senator John McCain, a strong supporter of the Geneva Convention rules for prisoners of war, has simply "caved" to the conservatives. As of this writing, Senator Arlen Specter (much to his chagrin) is battling to have even *habeus corpus* included among the rights of enemy combatants. So we should ponder on what has already been done, and what may continue to be done in extra-judicial organizations that somehow "transcend" human decency because of the utilitarian needs for social order, whether that be in the name of security or in the name of global capitalism.

It is precisely these utilitarian needs that reduce human beings to mere cogs in the machine of global capital and trade, whose hub and ultimate template is quickly becoming the evolving superpower nation-hive of China. It is this new world order that we need to examine in depth and comprehend for its values, so that we understand what is being challenged and what is being lost. If we don't understand this fundamental battle of values we will certainly put at risk all of the hard-won civil liberties from the Magna Carta moving forward, and in many cases propounded by philosophers since ancient Greece.

In a sense what is at stake is the fundamental definition of what human civilization is. Such a definition is by no means uniform and well-established, and is in fact still a work in progress. In the United States, humanistic tendencies and protection of individual rights are well-engrained in constitutional laws, enshrined in the Bill of Rights. We might take some time to read those rights. What they were understood to mean at their writing and what they mean now is at times in conflict. For example, the right to bear arms was primarily the right to bear arms against a potentially tyrannical government—yes, that means any government, including today's government—to ensure that it could be overthrown by force of arms if required. It was not, as some would have us believe, to protect hunters.

In the philosophies of the Asian East, notions of individual rights can seem to run counter to the humility required of Eastern thought, which sees the "individual" as illusory and as the precursor to self-centered, egotistical and ultimately self-destructive modes of behavior. In the East, and in many ways in the Islamic world, the Western notion of individualism simply leads to a decadent and ultimately corrupt focus on individual pleasure under the guise of "happiness."

The term "happiness" as the Founding Fathers understood it, however, is not the interpretation you might find in commercials for Gap Jeans or a McDonald's Happy Meal. Happiness, at its essence, can never be guaranteed. It is rather an ideal of what Professor Robinson at Oxford calls the "flourishing life"—the life well-lived according to the potentiality of that human being. And that potentiality might vary. But the idea was that happiness is the striving for individual perfection: emotional, spiritual, intellectual and material.

It is here that the Enlightenment of East and West meet, for the pursuit of perfection or enlightenment is the goal of both.

What has happened is that a few very intelligent people (mostly advertisers, political consultants and assorted zealots) have, over a period of decades, figured out how to co-opt the ideals and enlightened thinking of both East and West and turn them into fertile ground for manipulative mischief that trumps the spiritual, emotional, intellectual and even material wellbeing of the whole. While the enlightenment of the West becomes a pretext to justify a nihilism and hedonism used to promote a shallow, cynical, politically apathetic but shopping-friendly populace (we can look back to the Marquis de Sade and advertising for the roots of this trend), the enlightenment of the East is used to justify an anti-rationalism that fixates on swarm politics and sacrifices critical thinking at the altar of individual conformity—all for the sake or social order, security and the prosperity of the whole (we can look back to Mao Zedong and advertising for the roots of this trend). Both bastardizations of the enlightenment agenda can be found in the rhetoric of globalization and the realities of a rule of capital that is fundamentally fascist in its outlook. It is the rhetoric and rationale of advertising, pollsters and focus groups, of cynical linguistic manipulators for both the nihilistic hip and sound-bite fundamentalists, of fear and desire quite effectively massaged in the mindless march toward material progress. They leave in their wake incredible waste and destruction of the planet, and render many of its inhabitants not only unfulfilled but in a blanket state of perpetual—and perpetuated—misery. And all of this to make a few hundred billionaires. And we're all trying to buy that same lotto ticket which will never exist, when the real key to prosperity lies in vibrant local economies and entrepreneurship, not in the global hegemony of the Fortune 100. This anti-enlightenment agenda is actually quite simple: keep people stupid so you can control them.

It is the new world order based on the anti-enlightenment agenda and the rule of capital, the key word is of course "capital" and by inference the "market" (the "market" seeming somehow to exist as a thing unto itself outside of human activity). People have become slaves both to capital and the market, when in fact the opposite should be the case. Truth be told, markets and capital are a natural outflow of human inventiveness and freedom—which is the true source of prosperity—sustainable over the long term by an educated and aware populace. But not so, say globalization apologists, who explain that in this new order global capital and the market is a thing unto itself, a thing that has the ultimate power, freedom, and intelligence and must therefore trump the rights of mankind. It is the importance of this capital, and its movement, growth, and preservation that takes precedent over other judicial, moral, ethical, spiritual and even natural laws. In essence, we have created our new God, and He exercises his Will through the whims of the Market and of the movement of Global Trade and Currencies.

Can we stop this? Do we want to? Many of us, whether because we wear the uniform of the military or of the Fortune 500, may not want to. Moreover, the intelligence of the powers that run the system cannot be underestimated. The ecology of its mindset may so quickly co-opt idealism and altruism into a greedy free-for-all of consumer proliferation that it will leave our mind's spinning. So Bill Gates and Richard Branson beware. And a message to Bono and Madonna: an end to world poverty may not mean your CDs and music should eventually be sold to hungry Africans. A world of consumers based on the American model may in fact destroy the world through environmental meltdown. So global prosperity may in fact require that we move away from a consumer model and its values. This means global prosperity will require a massive rethinking about what both "poverty" and "prosperity" are. Poverty is, in fact, quite a relative thing: the lonely single person living in a "Mac-Mansion" in Fairfax, Virginia is as impoverished as the 10 illegal immigrants living in a small apartment in East Los Angeles. And the two types of poverty are intrinsically connected. A prosperous life may in fact be a happy one that provides for basic needs, but in tandem has an unlimited potential for mind, education, expressiveness and inventiveness.

Well, you ask, what then is the answer to the issues of poverty, globalization and environmental collapse that confront us? The purveyors of global capital, well-heeled and able to procure endless numbers of lawyers, gun-for-hire intellectuals, utilitarian economists and reductionist, myopic yes-men, must be fought with a simple and straightforward retaliation of common sense and reason. It is only reason, so well-loved by the Founding Fathers and the enlightenment agenda, that can crumble the system and expose in utter humiliation the bankruptcy of globalization's most pervasive ills. For it is reason—and a reaction to the assault on reason to take a phrase from Al Gore's upcoming book—that must prevail in order for the current system to adjust to the needs of the many and defeat the mad dash to cash out and provide the "golden parachutes" for the few.

It is reason, and an understanding that the global capitalist mindset being proposed as its alternative is intrinsically and fundamentally pathological and insane and will lead to eventual destruction of the planet and its inhabitants. It is this reason that will prevail or be lost and result in our downfall.

Morris Berman, in his seminal work *The Twilight of American Culture* notes that it is the defeat of the rational mind that ultimately leads to the downfall of civilizations. So it was with Rome; so it is becoming with the United States. The ills of globalization, understood intuitively by many people, are often reacted to emotionally and without a critical framework or common cause that could lead to a unified front or an alternative. This situation leads eventually to collapse and decay as the controlling élite lose their ability both to manipulate and sustain the dumbed-down, bread and circus masses with ever more debt-induced largesse. The piggy bank runs out as the underpinning rationality that must support any long-term prosperity gives way to the entropy of stupidity and fundamentalism, usually manifesting itself in some sort of inflationary bubble and/or war.

The élite, fearing an empowered mass of people, create the seeds of their own destruction by undermining the rational, disciplined, educated and humanistic underpinnings that gave rise to the prosperity they currently enjoy. Seeking to control the goose that laid the golden egg, they destroy it. If we owe our current prosperity to the wisdom of men alive over 200 years ago, we will owe economic collapse to the current crop of myopic lawyers, lobbyists and accountants that seem to run the show.

So progressives must come to love reason. They must unite, not under the guise of knee-jerk, emotional tit-for-tat politics, but go back to the fundamental notions that allowed this country to prosper and become great: rationality, moral freedom, humanistic tolerance, and an understanding of the need to balance the spiritual, the emotional and the physical with common sense laws that protect and promote the general welfare and not special interests.

It is still quite possible, should the will of the people be prodded enough, to change the current situation quite drastically so that a common sense, sustainable alternative to the globalization template is debated and implemented. In 1776, about 56 men got together and figured out how to start a country whose rational and humanistic basis allowed many people to prosper on many levels, to realize their own brand of happiness, until it got co-opted by the requirements of the American Empire and *Pax Americana*. We need to return to those times, to form our own version of a global Constitutional Convention, the one that took place from 1774 to 1789 in order to formulate the United States Constitution, controlled not by the myopic yes-men of capitalism, but by balanced, rational human beings (at least half of whom should be women and the majority of whom should be of color) with the intention of formulating a global system that will not destroy the whole as it continues to enrich the few. But the way out will not be through a single person—it can only be through collective action. This is what we need. This is what we must start in motion. And there is still time.

LOVING PARANOID MEDIA

(2006)

"The only real prison is fear, and the only real freedom is freedom from fear."
—Aung San Suu Kyi

One of the most interesting and pervasive trends in film and media has been an increasing sense of paranoia, both blatant and implied, in the messages communicated. The subtext of all this paranoia seems to rise from an overarching sense of apocalypse on some level, be that social, spiritual, environmental, or otherwise. In many ways, this sense of paranoia seems to be manufactured in order to keep media consumers in a heightened sense of anxiety and fear, because fear is, as any psychologist will tell you, the greatest motivator. In the case of media, that motivation is to watch, to be fascinated by the images and messages provided so that you, the viewer, are captured in the mental space of the media provider. The desired result is, as I will propose here, a vote or a purchase, and the more the better.

To be sure, a paranoid populace is more likely to cede power to those that can, in theory, remove their fear. If the government and corporate powers can make you feel a very real sense of anxiety, it's much easier to get you to get on board with a plethora of programs that expand their power and reach, or to buy the product and/or service that can (in theory) remove that fear and replace it with pleasure or stimulation. And the greater the *churn* of that stimulation the better: because it means you're buying more, not less.

Often, various paranoid media realities will play off one another, batting you around like a ping pong ball. If network television news pummels you with a sense of impending catastrophe, and you retreat to the Cinemaplex, what you see there will likely give you ample reason to feel more paranoid, not less. A common theme of horror and suspense films is: "Trust no one!" Return from the theater to the network primetime show, and you see more of the same: the crime drama. While in the past you may have turned to prayer and meditation for consolation against all these horrors, today you retreat to the iPod, which is at least corporate owned and profitable. Alternatively, you might actually embrace the paranoid and its stimulating media rush, and you wind up more like Freddy Kruger and less like *Friends*. Ultimately, we're all addicted in one way or another, constantly plugged into mediated realities which are controlled by promoters, advertisers, politicians and others who want a vote or a purchase.

What is missing is human interaction (don't most people spend most of their days in front of computer screens at work and at night, at home, in front of the TV?). God forbid you should want any quiet time on your own, or enjoy the normal pleasures of intimate human intercourse (particularly sexual intercourse, vile and rife with disease as that is). The fear of sex is used, strangely, to promote more of it, but again, of the virtual and porn industry kind that can be packaged and profited from. (As my mother once told me, sex has always been around, it's just that what people used to do in private is now sold on eBay.)

If you want to know how far we've ventured from what used to be considered normal human discourse, read Emerson's *Friendship*. You will note, if you're honest, that you probably have no friends based on Emerson's definition, because everyone in modern human society has become so commodified, demographied, slotted, digitized and consumerized (including our families), that human beings are becoming more like the Borg (of *Star Trek*) than anything else. (If you doubt this, try to communicate with a very focused computer gamer while they're in the zone.) Our purpose is to buy and sell, and other humans are just means to an end, equivalent to all the demonic forces in computer games you need to blast through to win the prize. In this reality, real estate and things (real or virtual) matter most, not people. Moreover, since most land has been spoken for and resources are getting scarcer, the only places ripe for economic expansion are either digital or, perversely, the human body itself. Why else would Americans be getting so fat, with fat oozing forth in places we never thought possible twenty years ago? Today's economic empires are not built on colonial expansion, but on the big bellies of couch potatoes, giving global expansion an entirely new meaning.

Hyper-consumerism, moreover, goes hand in hand with a paranoid media. Why? Because hyper-consumerism is fueled by over stimulation, which is best accomplished by shock and fear (or is it Shock and Awe?). Ask any behavioral psychologist: play classical music and the mice in the maze will go to sleep. Show them the CBS evening news and they will scurry around, agitated and looking for their next meal. And that, my friends, is the preferred behavior—to have us scurry to that next Happy Meal.

There was a time when the European Enlightenment (and its Eastern counterpart I would argue) offered us an alternative to our current form of hyper stimulated media fascination. That alternative is not mystical or obtuse: it's simply called *self-aware mature adulthood*, and everybody from Hollywood to Bollywood seems intent on keeping (mostly males) from achieving it. And what we have instead I will call media fascism because fascism has, at its root, the term fascination; in other words, fascination with power. For example, I was just in London, and witnessed the changing of the guard. Swarms of eager people crowded around to see behind the gates fascinated at the event and the emblems of power: the pomp and circumstance of royalty and its trappings. Just as we are fascinated by the Coat of Arms of the Royal Family, so we are fascinated by the Fox News banner and the unblinking eye contact of the news casters and the gowns at the Golden Globes and the Super Bowl half time. We give the providers of these experiences, in essence, our power and our responsibility: that is the transaction. They fascinate us, we give them power.

Of course the original model for all this fascination stuff is the church. The church used to be the primary mediator between us and God, taking away the painful responsibility of figuring out all this life and death nonsense and giving us the program, which, if adhered to, promised salvation. So it is today: but now the media and film is the church and the mediated reality is not God, but life itself, which is at its core (or so they tell us) a thing to be feared and mistrusted. What used to be called the "will of God" is now deemed "market forces"—and God's dark side, The Inquisition, has been replaced by *The Apprentice* and *Project Runway*. The alternative offered to actual living, painful and full of unpredictable outcomes, is the Mall, whose ultimate expression is Disneyland. Shopping is the ritual that has replaced churchgoing, the ritual that eases our pain by promising a buffered, safe environment of eternal suburban abundance. Abundance being, if you catch my drift, equated with heaven. Hell is, well, everything threatening that: terrorists, criminals, corrupt politicians, accidents, child molesters, calamities and, if you believe much of the media, most other human beings (keeps us from unionizing, doesn't it?). Heaven is the Mall—the Disney Experience—which gives us our myths and our purpose, but takes away our responsibility for figuring life out on our own.

If you doubt that normal human interchange is on the way out, just watch the Disney Channel very carefully. You will note that all of the teenage girls treat each other in in exactly the same way, furrow their eyebrows in a consistent and petulant fashion, and always have a little sound effect (like a cartoon) when they blink or a "swoosh" when they move. In short, most are not human beings, but witches or witches in progress. (Forget about Princesses, that is so old school.) The Disney answer is that we should all become like cartoons: that is, indestructible (soon possible with genetics?). And our leaders form the perfect example: Dick Cheney doesn't die, he has "a routine" heart episode which requires a quick fix and then, well, back up on his feet like Goofy in some Disney cartoon. The problem is that a lot of what Mr. Cheney promotes is not so funny.

Cartoon reality is the alternative to the fear and hell that supposedly exist everywhere else, and quickly becoming our idea of heaven. To find hell we need not look beyond CNN's *The Situation Room*. *The Situation Room* mimics a war room like mentality where there are multiple events occurring simultaneously in a crisis, and you, the viewer, are the commander in chief that needs to be kept abreast of all the incoming stimuli in order to make the best decision. The urgency propagated by *The Situation Room* and the 24 hour news cycle keeps us, in essence, in continual and anxious anticipation of the next event. The next event is, of course, the disaster waiting to happen. The next tsunami, the next terrorist attack, the next global epidemic, the next Katrina. Because if we are given a heads up we might, in theory, survive. (Ironically, many of these events are the result, directly or indirectly, of human activity.)

We might survive. If we stop and think about it a moment, the whole proposition becomes a little absurd when in reality none of us survive. We aren't really cartoons; I mean, we all die, right? Or am I missing something? Since we all die, then there must be another motivating factor behind all this urgency. It must be, maybe, yes I've got it—*we will survive longer than the next guy*. And it is surviving longer than the next guy that makes us the winners in a game where we all lose. (Look at the first winner of the *Survivor* show: he recently wound up arrested for tax evasion.)

Now you might ask, who the hell cares? I guess I do, so I ponder it. I ponder it because I am continually amazed at how manipulated people are by other (I guess more intelligent?) people who will do anything to optimize the system we have created that puts front and center as its core reason for being one thing and one thing alone: profit. That is, in essence, the value system that overrides all corporate decision making. Profit. Now profit isn't in itself "evil"—but when devoid of complementary motives (like common decency) and used as the fundamental driver of a society it can quickly skew reality in very interesting and perverse ways.

One of the more interesting reality alterations is that by commodifying a sense of paranoid urgency the capitalist system has, in its very real genius, figured out how to make money off our fear of death and our longing for immortality. Because the fear of death (if one looks at the philosophical underpinnings of such fear), invokes an urgency to live now and with a purpose; in other words, to live with a sense of urgency means to live with a sense that we can die at any moment, and therefore what counts is the moment. Then, once this is understood, the question becomes: what does one do with those moments in order to confront the continual fear of death that stalks every human being on the planet? Ideally, philosophers and spiritual teachers have us "live in the moment" and experience *heaven as life*. (If you wonder what I'm talking about, you might check out Terrence Malick's film *The New World*.) Marketers have twisted this ideal (along with many others) and channeled it to their own purposes. And it is here a funny little thing called *intention* comes into play. And, as Aristotle figured out a couple of thousand years ago, it is within the world of intention that all ethics arise. The intended "purpose" (according to Marketers) for our society is not that you should meditate on the inevitability of death and seek some kind of individual spiritual resolution or heightened poetic reverie; no, the intended answer for our society is that you should numb yourself to the reality of death through one of numerous distractions, hopefully several at the same time, and all of which are designed to make somebody some money.

However, a society whose intentions are, at its core, to selfishly seek one's own profit over another is a society whose days, one would guess, are numbered. This is the real apocalypse and the vicious cycle that haunts our modern culture. We feel our days are numbered because we innately know that the basis of our society is inherently corrupt because the intentions at its core are misguided (unless you're a true believer, in which case the ultimate good for society is profits). But the system, in its genius, turns that very sense of apocalyptic urgency into fuel for more profit, as everyone seeks to exploit one another and cash out on the sinking ship in ever more blatant and creative methods (like unnecessary wars). It is the cycle of our ever more cynical civilization: the sense of impending doom that surrounds us as our Empire implodes based on its own internal contradictions. In the case of the United States, social collapse will not, I assure you, happen without somebody making a lot of money.

If you doubt me, just take a peek at Jim Cramer's cable show *Mad Money*, as he cynically describes "government of the corporations, for the corporations, and by the corporations" even as he makes stock recommendations to investors.

So are our days numbered? The real novelty of our current system—what makes it different from, let's say, the Romans—is to perennially create a self-perpetuating social tension between our innate, internal, human ethics and an external, dehumanizing and invasive values that must seek, in some way, a release. And what if that release can be controlled, that desire to escape from the binary conflict that sees its manifestation in good vs. evil, heroes vs. terrorists, Republicans vs. Democrats, Red States vs. Blue States, Pro-Life vs. Abortion Rights, etc. etc., ad infinitum: in other words, *the perpetual struggle and conflict between opposites*. Our modern, technological twist is that all this struggle may not create chaos and decline: no, the tensions created between this struggle, exploited and amped up and in many ways created by a lot of clever people who control and manage the media message in highly Machiavellian ways—the result is energies channeled and released into hyper-consumerism. Yes, and then you've got real profit. Mega profit. Really huge mega profit. And we may not be doomed at all: *we just might be at the beginning of something really great!*

Understand, then, that our current method for social organization must create ever more tension and ever more paranoid urgency and ever more fear in order to create ever greater profits. Forget about peace. Peace is patently useless and must be avoided. The War in Iraq aside, even if in physical reality we have more peace (which is, in fact, the case, if you check the statistics), in our mediated realities we will have less and less as we move the reality of physical wars and crime to the reality of commodified virtual war and crime (meaning a computer games paradigm for living), of digitized and institutionalized neurosis and mental dysfunction and paranoia—a reality that is perceived to be necessary for increased stimulation and profits to create the churn necessary for hyper-consumer activity.

But there is an alternative: that the tables will turn on the reality manipulators in unforeseen ways in that individuals may seek release not in the shopping mall and computer games, but in self-awareness.

And there is a true urgency for such an awareness, because without it we may truly destroy ourselves (i.e., the environment has no reset button)—no matter how clever our leaders think they are as they play their games of social roulette. The urgency for awareness is the urgency of the individual seeking personal and social peace in a world which is determined in any way possible to remove that peace because that peace is, paradoxically, an affront against its (perceived) survival. You must be anxious, fearful, on edge and ready to deploy. If you are not you will perish, or so they wish you to believe.

But, as stated before, we all perish anyway. The question comes back to you, as an individual—how do you perish, your way or theirs?

LONGING FOR MAYBERRY

(2007)

"'I get it,' said the prisoner. 'Good Cop, Bad Cop, eh?'
'If you like.' said Vimes. 'But we're a bit short staffed here, so if I give you a cigarette would you mind kicking yourself in the teeth?'"
—Terry Pratchett, *Night Watch*

Before making my point here, I must admit having received three traffic-related tickets in the last three years in my home state of Maryland. The tickets came from a variety of policing agencies: state, county, municipal. I was required to take one day's worth of driving school or face having my license suspended. I took a 40-question test and that was that, unless of course I get another round of tickets. To be sure, I've become a better driver as a result.

I reflected a bit on this, at first wondering how and why my driving skills and/or luck had deteriorated so much in the recent past. I should note that in over 30 years of driving history, in general I've received about one ticket every five years. What changed?

What changed, I believe, was the aggressiveness of Maryland's law enforcement and the amount of officers in the field, and specifically the amount of officers assigned to traffic control. I'm not sure where all the money for all of these new cops came from. Probably a combination of healthy property taxes and Homeland Security. At any rate, I began to observe, and I don't believe I'm being paranoid, that at least in the state of Maryland there are significantly more uniformed officers willing and waiting to ensure that I do things correctly on the road and that if not they will certainly make sure I know about it.

Now my observations in Maryland are completely anecdotal, and it's not clear that statistics on what is called "force ratio" (number of police officers per thousand of population) for Maryland or in fact for the U.S. in general are kept and/or are maintained uniformly. My somewhat limited research indicates that a "force ratio" is normally about 2.5 per thousand in a normal suburban, peaceful situation. In cities, force ratios can be somewhat higher. In war zones, the force ratio of course goes even higher still. Military analysts believe that a force ratio of twenty-to-one is necessary to maintain control adequately of an occupied territory (such as it was with the British in Northern Ireland). Interestingly, the force ratio of Iraq is about ten-to-one or less. Some analysts indicate that a twenty-to-one force ratio in Iraq would require a force of about 500,000 troops.

My gut sense is that force ratio statistics (of police to population) in the U.S. would show a spike since 9/11, as law enforcement has ramped up with a combination of federal and local money.

Moreover, the attitude of law enforcement has noticeably changed.

In my youth, the ideal law enforcement officer was Andy of Mayberry. Law enforcement was conceived from a humanistic standpoint, that is, there was no enemy, only service to the population. That attitude has shifted. Now the enemy is everywhere and nowhere; terrorists could be anyone, and/or any "normal" looking individual could in fact prove to be the opposite, putting a law officer in danger. Hence the over-cautiousness of officers while approaching people in cars, even for minor traffic violations.

But while often understandable, this new attitude can also be overblown and disproportionate to the situation. The film *Babel* depicted perfectly the potentially over-reactive attitude of law enforcement to the population, in this case immigrant populations. At the border, the security guard in *Babel* enters into a confrontation with a young Mexican man driving the car in such a way that presumes guilt and promotes an adversarial attitude. The underlying subtext is paranoid and racist, nationalistic and protectionist. The border officer in some ways creates the very situation he is trying to avoid by prodding the "suspect" in a certain way. In this case, the young man panics and drives away in a hurry, prompting a chase that could have been avoided had the officers had a different attitude.

In my own case, the last traffic ticket I got was particularly frustrating, and I expressed it ever so slightly to the officer. I think I did something like briskly handing my license in such a way that I brushed his hand. The officer warned me that if I continued that behavior he would arrest me and charge me with assault on a police officer. I might also note that all this occurred on Christmas Eve—so much for "an officer of the peace" and Andy of Mayberry!

In airports, we are warned that even joking about bombs and other threats could land us in trouble. Danger is taken quite seriously, and apparently we are all potentially part of the problem. We are also, in a sense, recruited into a larger effort, drawn into the mindset of the military as they demand that we, in essence, understand that in "wartime" it is they that hold the authority, not us.

If you ever happen to watch the cable show "Cops" you'll also note that any higher force ratio of police officers is apparently aimed disproportionately at the homeless, the poor, high school dropouts and drug addicts. Many seem under-educated and clueless, like deer caught in the head lights of a very large Wal Mart truck. These shows, supposedly underpinned by the motive of "public awareness" are little more than an exposé on our growing inhumanity and cruelty. Not only do we *not* provide for the "criminals" in such a way that we could better their situation (like provide more educational opportunities), we laugh at them and use them as fodder for entertainment. We are throwing the homeless and underprivileged in the center of a media circus when we should be helping them. There is a growing sense of an unknown "we" that "they"—the police and the war machine—are protecting. This unease stems from the fact that many feel "we" are not always the people under protection. This is not to say that the motives and intent of law enforcement or "the troops" is bad—I'm not saying they are—but rather that leaders and policies must be buttressed by a vigilant awareness that democracy is fragile and can be eroded over time if the protectors of democracy lose sight of who they're serving, even if the motives of officers and service people remain essentially good.

This shift of attitude in law enforcement, subtle as it may seem, could bode ill for the future, particularly if more terrorist attacks and threats ever occur in the future—as they likely will. But it is a symptom of a larger problem. The real problem is political manipulation of the terrorist threat mindset, which along with another patently insane-as-normal idea, "mutual annihilation" popularized during the Cold War, take the cake for willfully unenlightened agendas touted by leaders as being both unifying and unquestionable. These agendas are put forth as an organizing principle of society, a society unified around fear. Fear then fuels the culture in such a perverse way that it becomes the lens of how a society views itself and, most importantly, a driver for economic growth. That fear should become a principle driver of wealth is a significant shift for the United States (remember that Roosevelt railed against it); we have always been considered such an optimistic country—one that is constantly looking forward, not succumbing to fear, either individually or collectively. Our entrepreneurial economy is, in fact, based on a collective optimism. If we lose it eventually we may lose our entrepreneurial drive.

Of course looking forward today means looking at what could be a rather bleak landscape of environmental collapse, ironically wrought in many ways by the very prosperity that was engendered through the optimism we embraced in the past. The issue is of course that optimism was channeled by some very intelligent (I guess!) people into ways to increase personal profit and wealth, and not as a rule in ways to increase the general welfare and/or individual enlightenment, and all at the expense of the environment. The result is that the United States' very laudable optimism, channeled as it has been for generations into primarily selfish activities, is a legacy of consumerism and shallowness that, when spread across the world, is not sustainable environmentally or, one could argue, psychologically. Virginia Tech and Columbine are woeful reminders of the price we pay, as is the War in Iraq. But more on that later.

Because our current economic system is not sustainable on a global scale, leaders must use diversions, like the War on Terror, to manipulate us in the short term while they ponder their options for creating new economic engines for capitalism to feed from—all, dangerously, based on fear. One option is to fuel economic growth via ramping up the "security state" (hence more cops on the street); another is to fuel economic growth by fighting the very ills we have created, mostly environmental; yet another is to fight illnesses (either real or created) for the body and mind (i.e., pharmaceuticals and biotechnology). Some politicians like Al Gore work to channel a society's energies in creative ways: the Internet, the fight for a clean environment. Strangely, what used in fact to be a dialog between left and right has become a debate on how to fuel economic growth, and which emotion to exploit in order to fuel it: fear or hope.

Historically, the expansion of capitalism has sought to be unfettered by the shackles of humanistic notions of social justice and equality, and equal distribution of the fruits of labor, as this will prove to be a disincentive to an economy driven primarily by the desire for personal gain. In fact, egalitarian talk (though also the basis for democracy) smacks the capitalist as too socialistic or worse, altruistic. The business of money is, after all, serious and pragmatic and, ultimately, classist and élitist. However, the language of business has been changing recently. The words "sustainable" and "green" pop up everywhere now. Corporate America, at least on paper, is embracing a "green" future and perhaps even an altruistic one. But buyer beware. Corporate interests have a funny way of turning things on their head: don't forget the irony of SUVs, for years touted as a way of getting closer to nature, advertisements always associating them with the freedom of the outdoors, with the underlying truth being that these vehicles destroy nature. Innate altruism, advertisers have long understood, can be manipulated.

Importantly, recent scientific studies have indeed shown that it is altruism, not selfish hoarding of personal wealth, that promotes happiness. The hoarding of wealth by the few (it is a well-known fact that 1% of the population holds up to 1/3 of the assets of this country) actually engenders an environment ripe for unhappiness—or looked at from another way, a society of dissatisfaction. It's not that people are unhappy—they aren't really happy or unhappy—rather they are dissatisfied. Dissatisfaction is, at its heart, the motivating principle behind consumerism, which requires a desire to be fulfilled temporarily and fleetingly, then fueled and/or created by advertising. The goal is to keep us incessantly in a state of ultimately unfulfilled desire, for that will create an engine for further consumption.

The consumer model is patently un-enlightened, as Western enlightened thinking guarantees us our right to seek happiness, not be manipulated into a state of chronic dissatisfaction. Here's the difference between the two ideas: one presumes happiness is attainable, while the other presumes it may be, but should be always kept just out of reach. Moreover, the mystical traditions of religion and Eastern Enlightenment actually promote metaphysical understanding where desire is transcended altogether and reality directly accepted. Therefore, the idea of anyone being enlightened on any level puts advertisers into an immediate panic attack.

It is chronic dissatisfaction that also leads to a culture ripe for situations like Iraq. While some will argue that Iraq is the result of a conspiracy, I will argue that it is more of a cultural event springing from generations of advertising-manipulated people and the heirs of those that thought up the consumer society in the first place: those able minds of the 1920s who mapped out how to manipulate people so effectively that they didn't even realize they were being manipulated.

Because the situation in Iraq springs out of a consumer culture, I'll call it the first consumer war supported by a willfully stupid ignorance of the facts. For one, it is a war that, whether consciously or not, is perpetuated by a low force ratio that keeps it in a continual state of chaos. Now be clear: I am not promoting a higher force ratio in Iraq at this time, although early in the war some unpopular generals indeed said we needed more troops, and were ignored. I am simply pointing out the fact that the way that the Iraq war has been conducted comes out of a consumer mindset and culture. How so?

First, the consumer mindset has it that the customer is always right. By extension, in our society, the customer is not only always right but the consumer of the product is always right. This particular attitude has been carried forward in such a way that literally hundreds or thousands of years of tradition of ancient societies have been discarded wholesale (as in Latin America and Asia) simply by the force of this idea and the "freedom" it touts. The idea is somewhat perversely associated with democratic individualism, which, I might add, has nothing to do with the customer being right, but more to do with individual responsibility. In China the notion of democracy doesn't even come into play: just buy and you'll be free, because after all you'll live the same way as the Americans do on television.

But back to Iraq. In this case the customer was Donald Rumsfeld, Dick Cheney and friends, including President Bush. The provider of the product is Boeing, Lockheed Martin, the Pentagon, the National Guard and assorted others. The customer, meaning the government, with consumer attitude in hand, dismissed the warnings of experts and instead listened to their short-term desire for instant gratification.

Moreover, being inculcated with the morality of advertising, they (consciously or unconsciously) created the perfect situation of perpetual war to feed a perpetual war machine: a consumer war that is unwinnable but great for the bottom line of all the companies involved, who in no way shape or form would question whether or not the customer was right, because the customer was, as would any good consumer, coming back for more product. And that, according to capitalism, is a good thing.

You will note on any product packaging that the provider always says you should use it at least twice. Shampoo especially. And Alka Seltzer. Using one Alka Seltzer is probably just about as good as using two; and shampooing once is probably just as good as shampooing twice. But that's not what is on the label. You always take two Alka Seltzer, and you always shampoo twice. And you always, by extension, have troops go back for more than one tour of duty. Because that way, you see, they use more products that can be replaced and bought.

In fact, cynics and conspiracy theorists have often pointed to Iraq as the perfect war for the MIC (Military Industrial Complex): long, with ambiguous end dates, well-funded but not funded so well to make it winnable. However, others will say that the Government is much too inept to think in this conspiratorial way. Such planning requires long term, strategic thinking, and, one could even argue, a little genius—none of which the Government in general possesses. This is why I said earlier that Iraq may in fact be as much a *cultural* event as a conspiratorial one; that the war in Iraq sprang naturally out of a consumer culture. That culture has it that from the consumer's standpoint they are king; and from the product provider's standpoint they want the consumer to keep buying more product. To this end, the provider creates a need. Once the need is created, a situation is engendered where the need cannot be removed.

In sum, the war in Iraq is a consumer war because it is the first war in which we have been convinced that we cannot do without it. The need has been created and now must be sustained. If we leave, we are told there will be chaos, even though we were responsible for creating that chaos in the first place. If we stay, there will be more death for Americans, problems with the national debt, the value of the currency and the sustainability of the National Guard. To ramp up the force ratio is impossible, because we don't have the military to sustain it and because we don't have an army of volunteers ready to line up to be service products—ah, sorry, service people.

This impossible situation is perfect for those that seek to profit from it. And the companies involved will continue to keep it that way for as long as the public remains willing to be stupid consumers and buy the goods they are being sold.

And for many people, that will be a long, long time. Or at least as long as they continue to shampoo twice. If things keep going the way they are, the label will soon say to shampoo five times, and we will do it.

THERE WILL BE BUCKS

(2007)

"Corporate Psychopaths are simply the roughly 1% of the population who are certifiably psychopathic and who work in corporations and other business organizations."—Professor Robert Hare

I'm not so sure that I really liked P.T. Anderson's *There Will Be Blood*. I do know the acting was superlative; or was it? I do know that the writing was top notch; or was it? The direction, while good, was not really that good. Or maybe it was really a masterpiece. I was not convinced, nor was I unconvinced. I did, after the end of the film, feel assaulted, but is that my problem, or P.T. Anderson's? One thing is for sure, though—the film was damn interesting.

Daniel Day-Lewis gave us a compelling character, to be sure, a larger than life portrait, one might say; or was it more a caricature of the late John Huston? The oilman Daniel Plainview most certainly was not necessarily a human being, and of course that may have been the intention. Or maybe not. P.T. Anderson is not known for moralizing, and it seems to me the titanic conflict between the preacher Eli Sunday (played by Paul Dana) and Daniel Plainview was more or less a revelation of some conflict within the psyche of P.T. Anderson himself and by inference, the American culture in general and the American male specifically. Ironically, it is the failure of *There Will Be Blood* as a drama that says as much about the American landscape as its supposed story-telling mastery. Mastery, I will define as art executed with results intended; mastery is not accidental, but contrived and well controlled. P.T. Anderson, like Quentin Tarantino, does not yet show mastery because he still seems to be struggling to master himself and does not understand the exigencies (and certainly not the value) of understatement. Moreover, both filmmakers feel as if they are pawns to some larger agenda and forces over which they have no control. Neither have very much perspective on or faith in humanity (not that they need it necessarily); as for Anderson, he apparently possesses a strong sense of the rage that must be expressed. Like the archetypal American, Anderson the person seems ultimately dissatisfied no matter how much material wealth and fame is heaped upon him, and can only cry out in despair through his art.

Drama in its most basic form involves conflict. We all took the course in college (or at least I hope so): man vs. nature, man vs. man, man vs. himself, etc. However, the ultimate goal of drama, according to the Greeks, is *catharsis*. Literally, *a cleansing*. One question that continually haunts me is whether or not we've lost the meaning of drama because of a slow devolution of what the essence of drama means that is happening in lock step with a more general dehumanization of culture that in turn flows in conjunction with the overall corporatization of everything. In a powerful, strange and circuitous way, *There Will Be Blood* reflects this. The result is not so much cathartic as terrorizing, toxic, manipulative and apocalyptic. But it could easily be argued that as a cultural shaman, Anderson is providing us with what we need: a sense of apocalypse that fuels some kind of introspection on the part of the viewer.

But I really don't feel any compassion in Anderson's agenda, nor should I; the bottom line is that Plainview's character is an emblem of how we are culturally redefining the human psyche (at least on screen) and the conflicts in the arena of human interaction in order to meet the requirements of modern society, with Anderson becoming an apologist for the cruelty of the market economy, and by inference, of nature itself. If human behavior is repeatable, definable, predictable, and manipulatable—largely by fear—well, then we have something that a market economy can deal with. To the extent that human beings are unpredictable, individual, chaotic, and existing outside of any common platform of understanding and don't respond well to negative stimuli, then they don't make such good consumers and are of less use to a profiteering agenda. To the extent that corporatization feeds on and influences human nature, it will tend to want people to be shallow, easily manipulated, predictable, and faddish. To the extent that people become that, we have sunk to the level of corporate tyranny. *There Will Be Blood* is a textbook as to how that can occur. But that does not necessarily make it a good drama.

As an altruist, I promote the idea that democracy (to the extent that we still have it), compassion and humanism can and should be an underlying cultural framework for stories. Such a storytelling methodology hinges on an underlying lack of cynicism and acceptance of the place of the storyteller in society. There is a term for a drama or a dramatic conflict that involves clichés, stereotypes, one-dimensional characters couched in cultural cynicism and so on: it's called *melodrama*. I'd argue that a lot of what used to be labeled melodrama is now called drama. We have in fact to a large extent lost touch with what good drama is because we have lost any belief that our culture can fuel it, revealed in the increasingly problematic role of the screenwriter in Hollywood (or the dramatic writer in general) and the growth of Reality Everything. Good drama, on display so well with the dramatic master William Shakespeare, hinges on the fact that human beings are ambiguous and not definable by strictly good and evil; and that ultimately all people are of value spiritually and/or humanistically. Good and evil, if they exist, work themselves out through shadings of anger, hatred, lust or conversely, compassion, love, sacrifice, equanimity and so on; in other words, the vices and virtues as expressed and in conflict within every individual to one degree or another. In my mind, Daniel Plainview is too narrow a sketch—too much of a line drawing and not enough of a fully shaded rendering. He is therefore not quite a character that rises to the level of the word *drama*. Nor does his journey provide a catharsis. Rather, his character simply outlasts and exhausts his competition. Plainview is, in a sense, the *uber apprentice*, Donald Trump on steroids. As such, Plainview has more affinity to a superhero cartoon than a human being; he is, in fact, sort of a *super anti-Hero.*

Today, many films that make it to the screen reflect the personalities of the producers who make them, albeit indirectly. They generally reflect cynicism and a lack of trust in storytelling as a necessary aspect of civilization. Because we have lost faith in our culture, our storytellers are suspect; we ridicule and interrupt the quiet we need surrounding the tribal fire that allows the story shaman to weave his magic. In an attempt to replace this lost magic, producers introduce violence as a means of subjugating an audience, rather than inviting them into what is an essentially spiritual effort.

After any significant exposure to the film industry one becomes aware of the fact that it is largely a producer's game. In what becomes an evolutionary process, writers and directors tend to give producers what they want: something that will make money. And from a producer's standpoint, it is better to have a smaller, consistent audience than a larger, inconsistent one. This is why they tend to like genres and sequels. Producers also tend to like stories of revenge. Having spent a little time commingling with producer types and competitive males in the film industry, I note that revenge, particularly in the United States, is a very real and very visceral motivator for many, because many are constantly being pummeled emotionally and psychologically (largely by rejection and/or by being ignored) on a variety of levels: by critics, by audiences, by agents, by stars, by conglomerate executives, by stockholders, and probably even by their wives and kids for not being enough—not famous enough, rich enough, *huge* enough. In a perpetual game of adolescent one-upsmanship, squashing a weak competitor is fun to some producers (or some businesspeople in general), a release, like squashing a bug in a video game. The result of competitive squashing is a numbing of the media producer/corporate man who must make these things and the creation of men (and a very few women) who are machines intent on doing one thing: making money. Toward this goal they use and discard anything they need to get the job done.

There Will Be Blood displays such a person in full dysfunctional glory—Daniel Plainview, in 'plain view' for all to see. It is about a man who only cares about money and power, like the producers who made it and the studios that shop it, or perhaps even like the filmmaker who directed it.

While *Gandhi* may have made it to the big screen 20 years ago, we glorify the shameless profiteer in this film and lift him to the heights of the godhead. Moreover, he beats the hell out of a weak, hypocritical moralist (Reverend Sunday) who must depend on his (Daniel Plainview's) largesse to survive. In fact, he does this to a lot of people, in an extreme fashion; thus he both shocks the audience and does not ultimately impact them because he is outside of their mode of conduct. He is more like a violent clown in a video game than a human being, albeit with intellectual pretensions. But the final message is simple. Existence precedes essence: the physical defines the spiritual, and not *vice versa*. The spiritual, in fact, is a cipher to the material. Thus the film is a materialist's revenge on the spiritual hypocrisy that has controlled much of western civilization. And we know who is in control when comparing the artists and the producers: the producers, of course. As advertisers say, "the reptilian mind always wins." Or so we are told to think, and we often do—thus creating the very reality intended.

Like another immortal question, that is, whether or not the universe is an essentially compassionate or adversarial place, *There Will Be Blood* asks us a similar question: Does spirit guide us or does the material? And ultimately, are the spiritual passions any different from the material passions; and does passion, at its core, simply reflect a will to power and dominate, whether or not that passion is spiritual or material in nature? Is the agenda of Christ, in fact, simply a will to dominate and "save" imperfect nature? Or is that the agenda of the Church, and not Christ, and thus the Church eventually has much more affinity to the corporate than the spiritual? Is the Church, working in conjunction with the Daniel Plainviews of the world, therefore the Anti-Christ? Is the corporate mind, whether through business or the Church, the 3rd Revelation of the Bible as touted by the preacher Eli Sunday? Is the Anti-Christ really dark minds working with each other in apparent unity?

In his titanic battle with the preacher, Daniel Plainview clearly wins, or does he? It is not known, really, when Plainview finished off the preacher with his final blow at the end of the film, what the statement "I am finished" means. It could simply mean that he is finished, like he is finished eating; he has now finished killing, and the servant can clean up accordingly. Or does it mean that he is finished because he has transgressed the laws, and will therefore be subject to the rule of law? Or does it mean he is God of Nature, and he has finished his handiwork by destroying the true evil of society: *the weak?* Or does it mean all of the above?

Moreover, there is something strikingly unusual—whether intended or not—about the character of Daniel Plainview that separates him from, let's say, a Citizen Kane or a Hamlet. He had no woman. He in fact appeared to be completely celibate, without interest in sex or women. Again, I'm not sure if this was intentional, but it was sure interesting. It was as if elements of Plainview's personality were developed dramatically that totally over-shadowed others, creating an imbalance that was similar to let's say, Edward Albee's *Who's Afraid Of Virginia Woolf,* where the young couple are so overshadowed and overpowered by the central characters of George and Martha played in the film version by Richard Burton and Elizabeth Taylor. This imbalance, however, makes Plainview's character unrealistic and bordering on caricature in the worst case or, more generously, insanity on parade—but again, this apparent dramatic imbalance is something that Albee was accused of in *Virginia Woolf.* Only here we see it within the development of a single character.

One could argue that as a result of his imbalance, his *Koyaanisqatsi,* Plainview has in him an overwhelming rage to dominate that completely obliterated anything hinting at the weak and feminine, except for the love of his son, who was, interestingly, not his son at all but merely a prop used by him to get what he wanted. He did, however, love his son—that is apparent; or at least he feared his deafness because it would reflect a weakness in himself, making his failure and lack of control all too apparent. So when his son becomes deaf, Plainview apparently loses his own ability to hear in the human sense, and the son simply becomes an emblem of that fact.

Anderson is essentially showcasing for us, through the character of Plainview (and whether he really wants to or not) the dysfunctional male psyche that has created our current world situation—or at least the one Anderson would like us to think he has. *There Will Be Blood* displays a man who almost seems to become a caricature by his own design, his own choice, by his own *will*. Thus Plainview is God as he redefines what it means to be human in his own inhumane, insensitive and angry image. He is, in a sense, the *Yahweh* or *Jehovah God* of the Old Testament: vengeful and destructive of the weak of flesh (maybe that's why Plainview had no sexual inclinations?) and perhaps, by inference the Compassion of Christ of the New Testament. We know that, and we respond with praise—perhaps because we doubt the veracity of the compassion, but not the *realpolitik* of the power. The result is, apparently, admiration for the latter and a tacit acceptance of its (often violent and inhumane) agenda. As such, this film becomes propaganda for the middle class who the System wants to maintain within its fold. Or is it propaganda? Perhaps our individual reaction to Plainview shows us the side of the moral question on which we sit. By walking this razor's edge, the film becomes a work of genius—and this is what makes it appealing across many audiences. It also makes it intimidating, and critics roll over on their hind legs as a result.

There Will Be Blood is like an anti-*Breaking the Waves* (director Lars Von Trier)—another film that dealt with Oil and the destruction of the feminine. However, rather than the Goddess Bess (played by Emily Watson) we have the Jehovah of Plainview, who is a producer's dream character, a glorified and artistic version of the profit motive brought to life in an Academy Award assured performance by D.D. Lewis.

When I saw Anderson's *Punch Drunk Love* at the Cannes Film Festival, I was similarly amazed at how dysfunctional Adam Sandler's character was: the festering rage that Anderson used both to comment on the culture and to dominate the viewer. Anderson was at once in and outside the character, something quite unique. Again, I'm not sure if it was intentional or not, but it was quite something to see. Plainview, I would call another Anderson dysfunctional male, and again a marvel to watch, but the result is a mere assault, whereas in *Breaking the Waves* the result was something transcendent. Thus again the film is a perfect contrast to the spiritual man's view of the world, and the perfect victory for the materialist and the producers of American films, and certainly to be heaped with Academy Awards.

Violence in our culture is commodified and used to dominate audiences in theaters—to literally "tame" an audience with violence, to kill their view of the artist as weak; the evolution is displayed in artists like Martin McDonagh, a playwright who went from the poetic humanism of *The Beauty Queen of Leenane* to the sheer, dark violence of *The Lieutenant of Inishmore*, where he emulated Quentin Tarantino (on stage in a bloody melee!) in an apparent ploy to get himself a film career (note his upcoming film *In Bruges*) and ensure audiences would submit. And it worked. He understood that producers are looking for such stuff because it reflects the mindset they have to assume to succeed in the film industry. Like *The Apprentice*—the definitive propaganda ploy of an amoral Capitalist mindset—the values of aggression, insensitivity, domination, fear and control are lifted up as the materialist's version of reality and the caricature of Donald Trump becomes what we want to emulate. Whereas 100 years ago a Martin McDonagh might have become a G.B. Shaw, today he becomes a Tarantino, a Donald Trump of filmdom.

Violence is used by filmmakers both to reveal their characters and pummel an increasingly numbed populace into feeling something where they can only be prodded into getting a hint of their remnant humanity if somebody on screen is walloping somebody else with a venom that would have made audiences fifty or even thirty years ago heave in the aisles. Violence today, even the "spiritually-justified" violence such as in *The Passion of the Christ*, has become pornographic and intimidating, a method of control. I'm not saying violence on screen is never justified—for the reality of life is that it is often violent; rather I'm suggesting that the hyper-violence we often see today both drives away audiences and drives out the diversity of human stories that would make film culture much more interesting.

But less hyper-violence doesn't seem to be the trend: the new sci-fi film *Cloverfield* is apparently trying to find a new boundary for today's excessive violence and terror with a *cinema-verité* like panache, to see where an audience can be taken and sets, apparently (I have not seen it) an even higher bar. This film, as well as *There Will Be Blood*, *No Country for Old Men* and *Sweeney Todd* seem to have taken the old standard that violence and aggression sells and elevated it to new heights.

On the other hand, whole swaths of audiences are left behind in this bloodbath. Capitalism, in its ecology of profit taken to the film industry, tends for producers to create films that reflect their own psyche that appeal to a limited niche that in turn is well trained, like rats in a maze (mostly a teenage maze) to return. These audiences are more likely to read graphic novels and Anime than William Shakespeare; and the Hollywood's business herd is chasing this audience with competitive overkill.

Moreover, the *style* of how much business is done in America (discounting some belated attempts at "green-ness") neatly dovetails with the content of its Hollywood movies, with the implication that psychological aggression and amorality is a prerequisite for doing business (a wholly silly notion in my opinion) drawing a clear line between those that have the stomach for competition and those that don't—the winners and the losers of our social hierarchies—as if winners and losers is all there can be, diverting us from what we really need: collaboration, organization and cooperation to solve the issues of the day and to make the great art of the future.

I'm not sure we can break this cycle until we have some sort of defining cultural upheaval, or if we ever can in the realm of the artistic (maybe there's some hope in politics!). However in my opinion we do need more options in movies, more artistic threads, more democratic choice, maybe just like we need more political parties. This is unlikely to happen unless there is a complete transformation of Western Culture (or Hollywood) or maybe a Writer's strike that never ends until the Iraq war does. Until then, the status quo will continue marching films (at least American ones) down this path: ever more violent, ever more melodramatic, ever the same and ever less human as the scions of capitalism try to mold us all (or in the case of Daniel Plainview, beat us all) into pliancy. Ultimately, the issue becomes one of self-worth, and the cycle is self-sustaining; people today in general do not feel very good about either themselves or the human race in general; the movies they choose to view give them little reason to feel otherwise. If people and movies and culture are to change, people must feel it, and they, are worth the effort.

EMERSON MEETS WALL STREET

(2009)

> "All life is an experiment. The more experiments you make the better."
> —Ralph Waldo Emerson

Recent economic turmoil begs the question of whether or not we've created, with globalization, a monster without limits—as Joe Biden would say "Wall Street Gone Wild." It seems a lot of intelligence combined with a great deal of greed has created an interesting financial box for the world to work itself out of. At work is an economic syndrome that cannot be looked at in black and white terms and is thus outside of the realm of most politician's tendency toward a mythic, good-guy/bad-guy outlook. Over the past 25 years, certainly since Reagan's term in office, we have been intent on dumbing down our politicians and our population during just the period when we most need them to be able to think. Yet, there is still hope, because enlightened thinking is no longer a luxury, but a requirement of survival as the world of high finance is being stripped bare of any vestige of credibility.

I'll explore here three areas that could lead us toward a more humane and enlightened economics. These are the power of systems thinking, the benefits of a citizen's dividend and/or basic income guarantee for all people, and the general concept of Economic Democracy. If, after reading this essay, you find the concepts intriguing, a quick Internet search on any of these terms can provide a good grounding, as well as a sense of the individuals promoting these ideas.

At the root of the current conundrum we face is our economic crisis. However, it is my feeling, and I believe many Obama supporters would agree with me, that the issues outside of our economy are of equal importance. Listing the most pressing would include: energy, the environment, poverty, debt addiction, and the failings of health care, and education to name but a few. And that is just within the United States. My sense is that to address the fundamental economic issues outside of the others would be a mistake, and that indeed we have a unique opportunity with this election to start on a path of sustainable economic growth that in fact enhances the environment, empowers individuals, creates "green" prosperity, enlarges the educational opportunities for our young people, and enables us to address the problems of health care. "But how" you ask "can we do all of this at once?"

First, we need to think systemically. There has in fact developed a powerful discipline in recent years surrounding systems thinking and, for lack of a better term, systems architecture, which can be applied to just about any set of human problems. One area where systems thinking and architecture has been aggressively applied to a very complex issue relates to aviation. The result of that architectural effort has been the Federal Government-led NextGen initiative that is 25 years in scope and deals with very complex modeling of relationships between private-public sector relationships, technology, the physical air space, and a myriad of other factors. This complex, interrelated and interdependent modeling effort has then resulted in a series of concrete changes and proposals for how aviation, air traffic control and the relationship between regulation and free markets can work most effectively. Run through the Joint Planning and Development Office (JPDO), this cross-agency effort can and should be replicated for the economy. What we need, in other words, is a Joint Economic Policy Office that coordinates economic policy between agencies, including Health and Human Services, Education, Environment, Housing, Labor and so on.

Such a cross-agency systems approach can and should be accomplished with our economic sphere in such a way so as to address the myriad of problems we have confronting us. So, for example, we should not make "knee jerk" responses in a linear fashion to our energy problems by freeing up all of the drilling off shore. To do so is not thinking systemically, as it is painfully obvious that fossil fuels are not the primary energy source of the future, i.e., they are not a viable sustainable energy solution. So why pursue that path if it is so obviously not a long-term option? A rigorous approach to systems thinking would eliminate what seem intuitively to be bad choices from our policy making process.

But doesn't this smack of central planning? It won't be as long as the primary goal is to develop policy, and policy by its nature is not intended to dictate the specifics of procedures and protocols, but rather to influence change.

Ultimately I believe systems thinking as related to the economy can lead us to an enlightened economics that frees us from our current plight of perpetual war, perpetual debt and perpetual prescriptions by seeing that solutions to war, economy, debt and ultimately even human and environmental health are inter-related.

As a first step, I believe that systems analysis must be applied to our current method of financing— how we use debt to finance the gap between what we can produce and what we can consume. I for one am convinced that what could result from such an analysis is some kind of minimum guaranteed income program that rewards the overall productivity of our society and world rather than "punishes" us through interest. This idea should be put through the rigors of systems analysis, along with many others, such as social investment programs, public-private banking, non-debt based money, intelligent taxation—all part and parcel of what the next wave of progressive policies that many call "Economic Democracy," an inkling of which is already showing up in legislation backed by the Bush administration as they push to solve the financial mess through social investment in private sector banking. Bush himself even coined the term "democratic capitalism" when referring to the agenda of the upcoming Bretton Woods-like economic summit (Bretton Woods being the financial confab in 1944 that defined the post WW II financial environment)—a series of meetings that will bring together world leaders in late 2008 (including President-elect Obama) in an attempt to shore up further a new approach to the economic crises.

The idea of a citizen dividend and/or basic income guarantee (aka, BIG) within the context of economic democracy assumes that all people have equal worth and that all individuals, simply by being born into the planet, should be able to live without, for lack of a better term, having to pay for the right to do so. Thus all eligible individuals should receive a BIG and/or dividend that would, over time, empower what is currently a perpetually indebted underclass. Over the long term, debt-addiction is unsustainable, as it ultimately leads to a society of debt-slaves, even if this was not the intended result. In the end we wind up with a society which is literally unable to function outside of debt and where everyone is caught in its web, even, strangely, many of the wealthy themselves. What needs to be questioned, therefore, is the validity of our current form of finance capitalism, and whether or not this is the only viable model at our disposal. If we decide on a different path, it is completely within our power to reorganize the debt relationships, nationalize our central banking, redefine our methods of valuing labor, rethink our ideas related to "productive" and "non-productive" endeavors in order to shift from debt-addiction to citizen ownership and economic empowerment. All of this could be done equitably, with currently wealthy individuals being compensated for any losses and in many ways benefiting enormously.

How do we afford this? First, revenues currently tagged for Social Security and unemployment would be moved to an overall BIG fund. Second, income tax for most individuals and families could be removed and replaced by other revenue sources, including an intelligent licensing and fee system for corporations (many use fees essentially to allow corporations to pay nominal fees for access to publicly-owned resources), coupled with a consumption tax and/or corporate assets tax that would allow the government to influence consumerism intelligently and/or invest in industries that provide a green-friendly and sustainable future. Moreover, above a certain level, individuals and families could still pay a progressive income tax (for example, families making over $250K a year). The fact of the matter is that a large swath of low-income persons already pays no income tax at all.

In addition to the revenue sources already mentioned, a citizen dividend could also be funded through government ownership of large percentages of the financial system (currently part of the Bush/Paulson financial plan!), essentially channeling those profits across a broader level of society—profits that had heretofore been limited to a minute percentage of the population. And should nationalization of the banking system prove untenable, taxing financial transactions could be.

Finally, we can work on an international level to create a regime of debt forgiveness for all nations, including industrialized nations such as the United States, in order to free future generations from the shackles of unsustainable levels of debt.

Wouldn't this all be inflationary? Well, if George Bush's policies have done anything, they have proven the resiliency of the modern, productive economy to inflation; Bush has, in fact, increased Federal spending more than all previous presidents combined, with relatively minor impact on inflation. To be sure, inflation can show up in economic bubbles (i.e., in stock or real estate), as we have just experienced—but a systems approach could model what those potential bubbles are and address potential problems with sound policy. The same level of analysis could be brought to bear on the international impact of such policies. But if we taxed intelligently, and channeled our resources from a war economy to a green and virtual one (i.e., the next level of the Internet), we could very well find ourselves with increased wealth, reduced deficits, massively reduced poverty and homelessness, and a much happier population that should be able to avoid to a great extent the downside of inflationary bubbles.

Would such a scheme actually cause more wealth? The recent economic stimulus package (2008) showed us an example: while GDP shot up by at least a couple of percentage points due to the stimulus totaling perhaps "a mere" U.S. $100 billion in Q_2 2008, during the same period massive injections of liquidity by the Federal

Reserve into the banks totaling hundreds of billions (through loans) did not serve to un-freeze the credit crisis because the banks did not loan the money; instead they hoarded the cash, and we were in recession by Q3. In short, people spend money out of necessity while institutions, if lacking direction, will tend to hoard cash out of fear. This behavior is a microcosm of what a larger move toward economic democracy could portend if we unleashed the power of a citizen dividend.

But do we "deserve" a basic income and/or dividend? According to Robert Reich in his book *Supercapitalism:*

> America is far more productive than it was 20 or 30 years ago, but most people haven't shared much in the bounty. Had median household income continued to grow at the same rate productivity grew over the last thirty years, the typical household would have earned $20,000 more in 2006 than it actually did.

Given these statistics, a $10,000 or even $20,000 a year citizen dividend begins to make sense.

At first, one might cringe that the idea of a citizen dividend and/or BIG is too socialistic and makes the people much too dependent on what is essentially a universal government handout. But in a technological age, the romanticized, agrarian-based self-reliance of some of our country's founding philosophers such as Thomas Jefferson and Henry David Thoreau is an ideal that can never be realized. A universal, no strings, guaranteed income could in fact create a kind of stable postmodern economic infrastructure that would actually enable self-reliance to flourish. To date, all efforts toward guaranteed income, including Social Security and a minimum wage, have been beneficial for the overall health of the economy; and Social Security has helped millions of retirees be more self-reliant. Why shouldn't a citizen dividend/BIG have the same kind of effect? By the way, early in the last century conservatives fought long and hard against both Social Security and the minimum wage, and certainly have been proven wrong on both fronts.

One of America's most influential (and underrated) philosophers, Ralph Waldo Emerson (the founder of the American Transcendentalism), would in fact be quite happy with a movement toward a citizen dividend, basic income guarantees and Economic Democracy, even though at first this might not seem intuitively evident. I mention Emerson because he is such an important and fundamental driver of many modern progressives, including (in the United States) Martin Luther King, Jr.. Emerson, along with David Thoreau, literally forged the unique idea of American individualism and self-reliance, the use of non-violence as a tool for change, and the need for education to be student-centered. And this student-centered approach to education is one of the primary reasons why American society is so well-regarded for creativity and innovation (it is also a tradition that according to writers like Chris Hedges is dangerously under assault by recent attempts to re-engineer education into something more useful to corporate interests). It is largely because Emerson and his colleagues stressed the right and need for individual awakening and the nurturing of the individual creative spirit that American society is so innovative and flexible. And it is because of the creativity and flexibility that we have fostered universities that remain, to this day, the best in the world and, one could argue, the direct result of the educational influences of the Boston intellectuals such as Dickinson, Alcott (both Bronson and his daughter Louisa May), and William Ellery Channing who were the contemporaries of Emerson.

Economic Democracy is simply an extension of the legacy of Emerson, Thoreau, Gandhi, Martin Luther King Jr. and others in the realm of economics (Gandhi, King and Thomas Paine in fact supported a guaranteed minimum income!), allowing us to create a bedrock of economic freedom and stability, enabling people to pursue a variety of individual goals outside of those that are "productive" in the eyes of those who control capital. By creating a guaranteed national citizen dividend, quite contrary to creating a citizenry content to "live off the dole" people would instead turn to a myriad of business, creative and personal pursuits that would in turn generate economic growth in areas fostered by the desires of individuals for personal fulfillment. This would ideally mean a movement toward green economics and virtual economics, and away from the shallow, consumerist, controlling and profiteering agendas of a the capitalist élite. While a majority of people would use the dividend as a supplement to a larger income (thus the idea of "living off the dole" is a myth), many would also pool their resources and begin, for example, communities dedicated to local and individual improvement, philosophy and the arts, alternative universities and media (all via a new level of the Internet, AKA Internet II), and a plethora of other enterprises as yet unknown that could be steered, with enlightened leadership, toward a sustainable future. Even if a section of the population chose simply to live off of their guaranteed income, those people would by design need to choose a simple, more environmentally friendly lifestyle—maybe not such a bad thing in our current age. Moreover, fewer people in the labor pool could force more innovation through more production software (empowered by Internet II) and other advances in technology, such as robotics.

Again, this is not socialism in the Soviet style. Why not? First, and foremost, while any dividend or BIG would be guaranteed, the government would not directly influence how it was spent, because unlike in Soviet-style socialism, government doesn't control the means of production. This makes it, in this sense, a market stimulus that would drive market demand. It is only because the American population has been force-fed by the current, corporate-owned media to fear anything hinting at the socialized, and because most truly progressive economic ideas are completely locked out of the debate within the mass media, that as a result that people are clueless as to their range of options. With the Internet and its democratization of ideas, many people have been supplementing their corporate media experience with Internet searches that broaden their perspective, allowing them to see that there are indeed alternatives to the current system of finance capitalism that is patently unsustainable, even in the eyes of a ten-year-old. Even some of the pundits of the corporate mass media are getting that point, whether it is Lou Dobbs or Glenn Beck of CNN or those within Fox News and MSNBC. And while Glenn Beck and Fox News would not necessarily support the ideas of Economic Democracy, they should certainly respect the choice of the people to head in that direction.

In short, many biases against so-called "socialist" ideas are cultural and the result of an implicit, long-term propaganda effort that allows the guardians of the economic status quo to control the range of and access to ideas via the media. Rather than trap people in the false promises of credit-laced prosperity, which creates an incredible reliance on the financial services sector, which demeans people over time, and which creates an ever-growing reality of income inequality, why not provide a no-strings applied grant or dividend that, coupled with an intelligent morphing of bankruptcy laws into debt forgiveness programs—including debt forgiveness on the national level—to be a de facto *investment in people* that will mitigate income disparities and, ironically, as described, create a better opportunity for *overall* prosperity than we currently have. We can look to the third world for micro-lending and grants as examples as to what people can do if given even a modicum of support and incentive. Moreover, it is precisely this investment in people and their potential that Emerson and Thoreau would support, because it is the power of the individual that they sought to unleash. Certainly Emerson would cringe if he were to learn that we launch our best, young, university-trained minds into the workforce and their post-educational life not with a sense of hope and opportunity, but often saddled with huge educational debt, sometimes mounting to hundreds of thousands of dollars!

The ideas of Economic Democracy will not eliminate individualism, self-reliance and capitalism. Rather, they will enhance individual potential and democratize capitalism, much as the Internet continues to democratize media, itself being an experiment in the power of individualism. And the result will be for the benefit of the many over the long term.

It is time we "reset" the world economy and shaped a new model of market-based, hybrid public-private social capitalism, and did it quickly for the sake of our long-term survival.

Martin Luther King Jr. spoke of this kind of hybrid or balanced economy:

Communism forgets that life is individual. Capitalism forgets that life is social, and the Kingdom of Brotherhood is found neither in the thesis of Communism nor the antithesis of Capitalism but in a higher synthesis. It is found in a higher synthesis that combines the truths of both.

And it is a stable synthesis of social and individual economic requirements that we should focus on moving forward, for our emphasis on the short term, while seeming to be quite the joy ride for some, has left the rest of us holding the proverbial bag. We might look back to Martin Luther King Jr., and forward to Barack Obama and Congressional progressives, for those ideas.

In 2006, the basic income guarantee was in fact proposed on the national level by State Representative Bob Filner (D-CA) as H.R. 5257, supported by author Matthew Rothschild. Moreover, economists such as John Kenneth Galbraith and even Milton Friedman have supported the idea of BIG.

We should move forward with these ideas now, and create an economic future for ourselves and our children that is worth living. I for one am sick of watching the DOW move up and down 500 points on a regular basis like some annoying child trying to constantly get my attention. It's time to wake up and smell the credit card offer for what it was and, as adults, introduce some much-needed maturity into the playground.

SUFFOCATING THE DREAM

(2010)

"If we are to teach real peace in this world, and if we are to carry on a real war against war, we shall have to begin with the children." —Gandhi

If there's one area where the blatant lack of fairness and sanity in our financial system shows its ugly face, it's with student loans. According to the Institute for College Access and Success the average college student amasses $24,000 in debt before graduating, a figure that has increased 6% from the year prior. Go to a private institution and that number can easily quadruple. At the same time, according to CNN, the unemployment rate for recent college graduates jumped from 5.8% in 2008 to 8.7% in 2009. A volatile brew of escalating tuition costs and a lousy economic environment are making young people rethink just how important a college education really is.

The result of all this debt is that many college grads are moving back home, living extremely restrictive lifestyles, or even considering leaving the country altogether. I read in one post where a young college grad, having gained acceptance into a prestigious university and become a hero in his home town, wound up $160,000 in private loans and now struggles with odd jobs to make the payments that eat up nearly 1/3 of his income. To make matters worse, the bank that was happy to lend him all that money is now under scrutiny for predatory lending practices, and the financial aid workers at his prestigious university are now accused of taking kickbacks. What a way to introduce an idealistic young person to the realities of American Society! Back in the 1980's, we might have heard about similarly coercive tactics used by the IMF when putting the squeeze on a third world country. Now the same mentality is finding fresh victims with 18-year-old mid-westerners from Iowa who are naive enough to sign up for a four-year program at an expensive school without any scholarship or money from their parents. Here's another good example from *Forbes.com:*

> Tamara Reese tried to make the most of college. After weighing various undergraduate programs in her home state of Ohio, she opted to attend the University of Findlay, a private four-year school with a price tag of $23,000 a year. The first person in her family to leave home for college, Reese double-majored in pre-veterinary medicine and biology, and was active in the school's theater and music communities.
>
> But eight years after graduation she isn't reaping the rewards of her hard work. Reese, now 30, faces student loan debt of $70,000—plus another $30,000 from graduate school in public health at Ohio State. Despite holding a series of jobs in academic research and at nonprofits, she struggles to make her monthly payments, which range from $600 to $900, depending on interest rates. Combined with the $250,000 her husband owes for medical school, the couple can't buy a house—and now they're grappling with the costs of a new baby. By the time Reese finishes paying it all off, her five-month-old son will be 26.

Now check this out. *Forbes.com* also writes articles advising students not to pay down their student loans but to instead invest (for example) $10,000 they've saved to purchase $20,000 worth of stock on margin. Now this is our American genius at work. Don't pay your loans, become a speculator like all the other miscreants on Wall Street, and beat the system by joining with the hedge funds in our collective speculative madness. And all of this is said with a straight face.

In fairness, investing is of course not evil, and professional degrees have always been expensive, so the return on investment can be well justified. But now we're seeing liberal arts students who get loaded up with outrageous amounts of debt, sold private loans in a predatory fashion, only to hit the job market and experience a quick dose of financial reality. We have to inject some common sense and balance into the situation.

What is clear is that the free-wheeling, over-leveraged, derivatives-addicted financial system is eroding the value systems that make for a society that can adequately call itself human. We shiest our children out of tens of thousands of dollars, pray that their good upbringing will keep them in line so they make their payments, and offer the carrot of speculation to win the lotto and get out of debt in a hurry. The values of such a system put a lot of pressure on basically good people either to opt out or to opt in to a kind of tenant farmer relationship with the banks. Because the reality is that we can't all speculate ourselves to riches—the numbers don't work out over the long term, and somebody ends up holding the bag (yeah, only the stupid people, right?).

The more likely scenario to speculative riches is that you find yourself in a lifetime relationship with banks—because the mindset of the banks is to keep you on the leash forever. While this might be "just the way it is" for adults, for our young people my vote is to forgive this student debt, and do it quickly. And while the recently passed Student Loan Reform (a subset of the Health Care Reform of 2010) will help young people get better terms for their loans and eliminate abusive private loans, we really need to go beyond a loan system and move toward expanding grants and debt forgiveness. To sum up, get rid of a couple of bomber programs, don't send tanks to Afghanistan, cut the President's pay—do anything—but don't continue to force kids into debt slavery so early in life.

TIME FOR EXOPOLITICS?

(2010)

"We cannot go forward as a civilization at all if we become a 'united earth' standing against other worlds." —Dr. Steven Greer

Certainly one of the most pervasive impacts of the Internet is that it has enabled people to get more directly at the truth. And yet to its detractors, it has simply given people the ability to parade their delusions effectively, and to global audiences. Regardless of what side of this argument you fall on, it's apparent that the Internet has forever changed how we consume information. And while the Masters of Traditional Media steadfastly believe that they have a basic level of control over the popular mindscape, and can mold it accordingly, that is changing quickly. So quickly, in fact, that this decade may indeed find the rug pulled out from under broadcast and cable media's proverbial Nielsen ratings.

Case in point is the *Zeitgeist* film. Distributed virally and free over the Internet, *Zeitgeist* has reached (some estimate) over 50 million viewers. And talk to anyone about YouTube. Put a relatively interesting video on YouTube and you can get 100K independent views. People watch this stuff.

But probably the most important, and salient, impact of the web on viral public opinion-shaping may be the UFO phenomena. An entirely new intellectual discipline, called Exopolitics (the political implications of Extraterrestrial presence), has evolved and begun to turn the litany of UFO "sightings" and whistleblower testimony into a rational—albeit radical—world view. When I say "rational" I mean that there is a rapidly developing framework that pieces together many conspiratorial threads in such a way as to create a narrative that may, over time, replace what one might call the Walter Cronkite world view that existed from the end of WW II through 2001 (i.e., 9/11). What started as conspiratorial rants on the Internet has now even reached mainstream cable.

Specifically, in May, 2010, the History Channel broadcast ideas about "Ancient Aliens" that a few years back would even shock the most loopy and glassy-eyed teenager, conjecturing with a straight face about some fairly outlandish arguments. And yet when these arguments (some that are quite compelling) are pieced together, they begin to create an overarching framework that forces any open and rational mind into a deep consideration. Is everything discussed by the History Channel true? Probably not. Is the subject worth looking at? I'd say yes. And much of the History Channel's line of thinking mirrors an Exopolitical checklist for UFO disclosure.

If you take the Exopolitical viewpoint seriously, U.S. policy has been directly or indirectly shaped by the ET phenomenon for the past 50 years, mostly due to the Government's cover-up regarding what it knows and the technology developed as a result. The technologies, and the resulting impact on our Newtonian world view, could be nothing short of profound in terms of its impact on the fields of aviation, energy and health. The problem is that ET involvement in world affairs may just prove to be an extension of mankind's need for a savior, when indeed we should be saving ourselves. But at some point, the question of "we" becomes diffuse—i.e., what constitutes the human family? I'll leave it to you to research and uncover what I mean by that.

All of that said, for me there are four incidents that gnaw at my sensibilities, and, if taken at face value and pondered seriously by our Government, should warrant immediate Congressional investigations. Some may in fact involve the Government—or factions within it—in an attempt slowly to open up the public consciousness.

These events, combined with the still-unanswered questions regarding 9/11 (the so-called "Truth Movement") and deep questioning of the veracity of our economic system, form the three most powerful virally-driven social ideas powering much of what is coming to be an alternative universe to the Cronkite View.

My sense is that after a certain critical mass is reached—perhaps prodded by some form of government disclosure regarding UFOs or a crisis (or both)—that the Cronkite View will "flip" and we will find ourselves in a different paradigm. By that time, Google TV will rule the world, and people will be pulling information from a completely alternative universe than is currently pushed (some might say foisted) upon us by Old Media. Enter the New Media Age. Whether that is an age of Darkness or Enlightenment will be up to us.

But what are these four events? First, the 1952 UFO "flyby" over Washington DC. Second, the "Phoenix Lights" incident of 1997. Third, the Stephenville, TX UFO sighting of 2008. And finally, the O'Hare Airport UFO incident of 2006. All of these events can easily be searched online. Forget about any extraneous and often delusional meanderings and mis-information, I urge people to focus on these events alone, which if taken at face value must make us all pause and wonder if we are indeed not alone. For me, after taking a hard look into these events I see good reason to give Exopolitics serious consideration.

Now the "game changer event" (known within the world of Exopolitics as the Full Disclosure of what the U.S. Government knows about the UFO phenomenon) may or may not occur within our lifetimes. What is most certainly going to happen, even if our galactic friends do not land on the White House lawn in the near future, is that we will discover Earth Worlds through our more powerful observation satellites, and that this will happen perhaps even this year, all via the new Kepler probe launched in early 2010.

So who are the key players in this Exopolitical landscape?

One of the most prolific writers in the Exopolitical World is Michael Salla. Professor Salla formerly taught at the American University but was booted out when he tried to take Exopolitics to the next level there, and legitimize the discussion. Suffice it to say his colleagues did not like what he was trying to do and he was forced into early retirement in 2004.

Now (again as of May, 2010) that no less than the renowned physicist Stephen Hawking has begun to chime in on Extraterrestrial issues and the implications thereof, the American University should consider hiring Salla back, and making him Dean of a newly minted academic discipline. According to Hawking, we can surmise that Exopolitics is a perfectly rational debate.

Salla, who along with others such as Dr. Steven Greer and Stephen Bassett, now speaks and writes passionately and independently on the subject. In 2008, Salla detailed a supposedly secret meeting that occurred at the UN earlier that year and involved a multi-nation discussion about the UFO phenomenon, and a new stance that governments were going to take, with an eye toward slowly disclosing the facts over time. I was surprised and amazed to see events unfold just as presaged by this secret event that was revealed to Salla by an informant he called "Source A." Like clockwork, countries began to release substantial information regarding their (mostly) military and "credible" encounters with unidentified craft. While some have recently questioned the veracity (and even legality) of Salla's so-called "Source A," it is clear that several countries did in fact disclose their UFO evidence in quick succession after the supposed UN meeting—and this is all well-documented. If "Source A" is a hoax, then France, Sweden, and the UK weren't listening. Even the Vatican chimed in and said the ET's were compatible with Christianity.

In late 2009, Salla wrote an article where he predicted that "Disclosure was imminent" and that in late 2009, or early 2010, the Big Cheese—i.e., the USA—would begin its own disclosure process that would echo those of the several European countries already mentioned. While this has yet to come true, there is certainly a sea change in how the Obama administration is handling confidential information; Obama has in fact created a National Declassification Center that has been ordered to begin de-classifying Cold War era records that are judged no longer to be a national threat.

It could be that this process will reveal the truth about UFO-related events that happened decades ago, so they can be discussed in a new light and with new information. This, along with discoveries of Earth-like Worlds by Kepler could be the final preparatory step prior to full disclosure.

One caveat to this neat argument is that there are (apparently) forces that do not want any of this to come about. The numbers of those lending credence to this are increasing. One example of this blowback may be the recent outing of Salla's "Source A" mentioned previously.

Call these forces what you will—the Shadow Government or Oligarchs or MJ 12—but certainly it becomes apparent to many people that our world is in some sense in a herculean struggle between a fantasy created for consumption on many levels—physical, mental, even spiritual—and a new paradigm trying to evolve. And the people that create this fantasy are not even remotely interested in us (or themselves) evolving. As your best friend would write on your High School Yearbook, so the oligarchs insist, "Don't Change." As such, they'd much rather have you obsessing over "Dancing with the Stars" than reading this article. Or worse, they might be fostering a climate for perpetual war.

At the end of the day, we as a human race must evolve. We cannot sustain our current destructive mindset, witnessed on a variety of levels in a variety of ways, and harmful to both the planet and ourselves. Some very clever people devised a system that is the equivalent of a one-way bungee jump where there is a flaw in the rope—some might say someone even cut it. Given that the U.S. Government spends ten times the amount of money on its military than its nearest competitor (China), and yet has 1/3 of the people, something seems out of balance.

I urge everyone to pause, to think about and to research the Exopolitical and Disclosure movement, and act as you think you need to ensure our collective truthfulness. Then communicate what you think to your friends and family. We may need to look at one another more and more for answers, and help, as we ascend what could be the slippery, but hopeful, slope of world change that could very well have an exopolitical component.

    As Gandhi said, "Be the change you seek." We may not have time to wait for Obama.

JUDGMENT AT NUREMBERG

(2010)

"Naturally the common people don't want war: Neither in Russia, nor in England, nor for that matter in Germany. That is understood. But, after all, it is the leaders of the country who determine the policy and it is always a simple matter to drag the people along, whether it is a democracy, or a fascist dictatorship, or a parliament, or a communist dictatorship. ... voice or no voice, the people can always be brought to the bidding of the leaders. That is easy. All you have to do is tell them they are being attacked, and denounce the peacemakers for lack of patriotism and exposing the country to danger. It works the same in any country." —Goering

Viewing Stanley Kramer and Abby Mann's *Judgment at Nuremberg*, almost 40 years after the film was made and over 60 years since the proceedings on which it was based have taken place, proved illuminating to me on a few levels. First, the film shows that an intelligent and nuanced discussion of the issues surrounding World War II were and still are possible, and second, that Spencer Tracy is perhaps the greatest film actor to have ever lived.

As for the first point, let's turn for a moment to the recent fall from grace of Helen Thomas. Helen Thomas, who served for many, many years as a celebrated journalist, is summarily judged and executed (to the extent we can do so today) for making remarks about Israel that are deemed, by conventional wisdom, to be disdainful at best and downright perverse at worse—bordering it would seem on moral depravity. Absent from the Helen Thomas media judgment, her subsequent apology and the universal assumption that she was completely off her rocker, was a nuanced discussion of her statements, and any analysis of those statements that would have contextualized them. To get such a contextualization we need to turn away from ABC, CBS and CNN, and toward *Judgment at Nuremberg*.

As for Helen Thomas' views, there are at least a few Orthodox Jews that actually voice the exact same opinion that Helen had regarding how the "Jews should get the hell out of Palestine." These Jews, apparently in the minority (I have not researched this) quite literally would support every iota of Helen Thomas' viewpoint. Now, since I myself have befriended, roomed with, worked for, and loved those of the Jewish faith and/or culture I don't think I am a good candidate for either anti-Semitism nor an educated discussion on the veracity of Zionism. However, I can say what I see—and what I see is that the mainstream media is utterly incapable of entering into a rational, even-handed debate regarding the validity of the Jewish State's position against Palestine, and the efficacy of the Jewish State as the solution to the issues surrounding World War II.

That said, such a debate was not the point of *Judgment at Nuremberg*, although the Helen Thomas incident underscores how World War II continues to be a pervasive event surrounding the American psyche, because the extension of that war exists with us to this day. If any war could have been said not to have ended, it is that war.

What was the point—or points—of *Judgment at Nuremberg*? Let me try to summarize them here. First, that a level of personal responsibility lies with all people for the atrocities that are committed by their leaders. Second, that this moral responsibility grows out of a fundamental understanding that all human beings are of value and are therefore due to be treated with equal justice based on the rule of law. And third, that large crimes begin with small ones.

Burt Lancaster's character Ernst Janning asks Judge Dan Haywood (Spencer Tracy) at the end of the film (I paraphrase): "You must believe me that I did not know that it would come to what it came to." As for Haywood, he replies: "After the first murder of the first innocent allowed, you knew what it would come to." Such words can be echoed today to any American, any person who allows atrocities to continue without speaking up.

In his closing remarks, Tracy's Haywood stated quite eloquently that "every human being is of essential value." Why was that important? It was important because it is only in dehumanizing others that atrocities can occur in the name of the State. This can happen today on many levels in many guises, and is a disease of which humanity seems ill-prepared to rid itself, although there are those that continue to try to raise the rationality of humanism above fascism.

Finally, large crimes begin with small ones. It is the first compromise that leads to the larger one, that leads to the massive crime. We can look to our recent financial failings for examples. Take Bernard Madoff, or Enron, or shaky derivatives deals. All begin with rationalizations, excuses, small crimes and cutting corners. Eventually, the whole society is rotting and a culture of corruption, buttressed by a fundamental dehumanization of self and others, takes hold.

Who judges the judges? That becomes a searing question for us, as Americans, today, posed by *Judgment at Nuremberg*, where American judges quite literally sat in judgment of their Nazi counterparts. Where are those judges today? Many that voted for Barack Obama had prayed and hoped for some kind of resolution to questions of Iraq, open questions regarding 9/11, and a real debate regarding the veracity of our financial system. Questions that could be explored and debated in the light of day by a people's tribunal of sorts, so perhaps we could begin the process of healing and transcending what we know are probably crimes against humanity, committed not by Nazis but by ourselves, who have become in essence the criminals, either directly or indirectly.

What occurs with the national psyche, just as with the individual psyche, is that this corruption, when not illuminated, when not brought to light and justice, festers and expresses itself in another way. And what better a symbol of that expression than the current Oil Spill. The toxicity of our system is literally washing up on our shores.

Do we address the internal toxicity that leads to the external?

It seems not. For there are questions of country, questions of jobs, questions of money, questions of practicality, questions of "the survival of the country" that arise to dissuade us when people desire such a truth and reconciliation movement. Arguments about "survival" were made by all of the men and women who compromised Germany at the time of the Nazis, who were themselves seen by most as the only viable vehicle for national salvation.

Where is our truth and reconciliation committee? Where is our *Judgment at Nuremberg*? While we are constantly told "not to forget" the atrocities of World War II and 9/11, what of other atrocities that occurred yesterday? What of the dozens of innocents killed by un-manned drones in Afghanistan? What of the hundreds of thousands of Iraqi civilians killed for no reason in the last 10 years? What of Rachel Corrie being bulldozed in Palestine? What of the monks being tortured in Chinese-occupied Tibet? We justifiably hold the emblem and horrible reality of the Jewish Holocaust as that which we will "not forget." And yet every day we are encouraged to forget other atrocities because they do not serve our interests. But what of the human interest? What of the interests of justice?

But we are in a new era. This new era has no Spencer Tracy, apparently—who himself, in reality, was just an actor, a myth of our own purity. Myth or not, we have no wise old men, for they are corrupted, or corruptible. We have no Sam Ervin, who led the Watergate Committee. What the powers that be do not understand is that we are destroying ourselves by not allowing ourselves the transparent self-criticism that we need with Iraq, with 9/11, with the financial system, and with other issues. It is impossible for a rational human being to exist in this situation, knowing what they know, and not to demand justice on some fundamental level. Without it we wither and we end up with the type of justice we provided Helen Thomas, who, like Spencer Tracy's wisdom, is apparently an anachronism, and easily discarded as we move on to the next news cycle. A news cycle that seems strangely to conspire against our awareness, even as its false sense of urgency touts its importance to us all. Wisdom is lost, the type of wisdom seen in Spencer Tracy's Dan Haywood.

And yes, Spencer Tracy. What is it about the man? He was, after all, just an actor. Apparently he was a flawed man. But there was greatness about him, and certainly greatness in his acting, an honesty, a transparency into the inside of the man, his weariness and his burdens. It would do us all good to look at *Judgment at Nuremberg* again and again, to look into the craggy face of Spencer Tracy and recognize that if we can imagine such a man, such a wise man, that we as human beings, by the very force of that imagination, may be able to find our way out of the round of delusion and myth we seem so content to live with. To imagine, indeed to find, some measure of justice and enlightenment, in these days where such things seem so passé, so impossible, and yet, so needed.

We elected a Black Man, hoping he would replace our lost Spencer Tracy. Certainly he is up to the task. However, it also seems to me that he, our President, is not listening to what people crave. He is not seeing what we need as a nation. We need truth. We do not need to know whose "ass to kick" regarding the BP oil spill, for that is tangential to the real issue: that we are lying to ourselves, and getting rather used to it.

DIGITAL MORALITY

(2011)

"Mankind's universal values of love, compassion, solidarity, caring and tolerance should form the basis for [a] global ethic which should permeate culture, politics, trade, religion and philosophy." —Wangari Maathai

We live in an age of technology, and every day we interface with technology more and more. In fact, many of us interface more with technology than we do with people. We engage in online chats, comments, feedback, emails, texting, computer games, movies, cable, television—the list is endless. We live in a mediated space that is corporate owned. Ostensibly, we are wired into this digital space for our benefit, to allow us to connect with our fellow human beings more efficiently and effectively. But is something lost in the process? Are we becoming consequently different as human beings?

I will argue we are changing, and that interfacing with so many machines and computers is molding us in their image. The values of these technical devices are beginning to trump human values. We tend to value speed, efficiency, accuracy, promptness, and utility over patience, generosity, and empathy. Rather than machines serving mankind, we wind up serving the machines instead, or changing our behavior and ethics to suit their reality. As a result, we admire the latest iPad more than the greatest acts of altruism.

Our country's recent financial struggles highlight this new digital morality. Rather than being guided by "the golden rule" where we should "do unto others as we would have them do unto us," many of our financial institutions and other businesses take another, more self-serving tack. The credo becomes instead "do whatever is legally allowed and that provides the company the greatest benefit/profit." Computers, designed for efficiency, are implicitly guided by this same morality. The computer's task, "business rules" and workflow take precedence over a broader question of the impact of that task on the wider world. The narrow, legalistic, rule-based and specialized world of the computer becomes the moral space not only for our businesses, but also for our lives. Lacking a more holistic view, we are concerned for our narrow, specialized existences and their narrow, specialized concerns. Our morning routines mimic the work flows and processes we strive to perfect at work. We settle into these routines as if to protect us and shield us from something, and become as numb as the machines that do not feel or think about their particular objective. We simply perform the routine, fulfill the task, and repeat. To paraphrase Charlie Chaplin from his speech in *The Great Dictator*, we become "machine people with machine hearts."

When we judge, we judge harshly. Software, which will "crash" based on a single typo in a computer program, becomes the emblem of our judgment of others. The recent fall from grace of Representative Weiner is one example. It was a "typo" in a text message that "caused the chain of events" that led to his fall. As such, single failures tend to prove disastrous for otherwise good people. While Representative Weiner may deserve his fall from grace, we take this same kind of morality too far when we judge people based on a single action out of context and do not look at the wider picture. We don't ask, "Who is the judge"? Instead, we assume there is some pervasive, mass morality where everyone uniformly dislikes certain behavior and avoids that behavior with puritanical zeal. Is this really the case? I am doubtful. We will find instead that we are all flawed, and none can cast the first stone.

Again, we view people's actions as software—where the single flaw causes the whole system to crash. This kind of morality actually has us believe that to choose between saying "oh my gosh" and "oh my god" is a profound moral choice, even as we blithely buy from Costco products manufactured by day laborers that slave 14 hours a day for sub-standard wages, some even with *no wages as real slaves* from jails in Asia! But neither they, nor we, are software or machines, and none should be judged as such. In fact, our own jails are filled with people who probably would be better off in rehabilitation, being forgiven and re-integrated into society rather than judged for "flaws" that are as much the result of systemic, societal problems as their own doing.

The machine or computer task, isolated and specialized, becomes the human being, isolated and responsible for their actions, and devoid of context—all while plugged into their digital space. The infallible "perfect" ones who do not fall into the trap of "error" can judge those that commit crimes and are jailed when, truth be told, a more humane approach would work better over the longer haul. And this attitude reaches much wider than the criminal and deep into our personal lives. Often these "perfect" ones are not the most empathetic, but the ones with the best credit scores, whose efficiency at paying their bills makes them somehow "better" than the "failures" who have, perhaps due to illness or other misfortune, allowed their credit ratings to lapse.

We live in rows of houses where neighbors more often than not do not communicate. The suburb becomes not so much a community as a compartmentalized, specialized human chicken coop. With many of these houses financially under water, the people in them feel more trapped than ever. Terrified of losing their credit rating, they keep on plugging away at the routines of their lives, hoping there will be an exit and praying they don't fall ill or lose their job.

Our children often interface more with computer games than with other children. The values of these games are of domination, control, and aggression. The values of cooperation, empathy, and collaboration are farthest from the minds of most video games creators. Our children, immersed in a "squash the bug" mentality, take this morality out into the wider world. The answer to all problems is to "kill the enemy"—fix the problem by eliminating the dehumanized "other" who is at the heart of our unhappiness.

Am I being too harsh? I am certainly exaggerating the problems, which are much more diverse and balanced than what is portrayed here. But I do so to make a point, and I hope you see that the trends I'm pointing out are very real, and leading us toward a society that could, within a hundred years, be completely unrecognizable as human culture.

Do we want a future of hybrid robot-humans? That is where we are heading. If we want to stop these trends, the only answer may not be more and more machine values with their digital morality. The answer may be to rediscover our humanity.

THE TREE OF LIFE

(2011)

"I believe we are on the edge of a quantum leap into a whole new way of organizing and living as a human family." —Mairead Corrigan Maguire

Seeing Terrence Malick's *The Tree of Life* was in a sense a return, because I had my film debut about ten years ago prior in the same lower east side New York City neighborhood where I wound up seeing *Tree of Life* this past week. Since both Malick and I seem to be inspired by a similar vision of film, and since both of us (apparently) trace much of that back to Italian director Michelangelo Antonioni, it was almost as if I was watching an extension of Antonioni—as if Malick's film was indeed another branch of an ever-growing tree. While I'm not sure if Malick has ever seen my own Antonioni-inspired *Clouds*, I found it striking that we came to similar conclusions about life and the expression of life through art, albeit via completely different paths.

As such, seeing *Tree of Life* was deeply personal and made me feel somewhat vindicated about the artistic choices in my own work—whether that be in film or the criticism thereof. With *Tree of Life*, Malick is expressing very much what I propose as an alternative direction in film style in an essay titled "Peace as Style," where I discuss Antonioni as being the precursor to such a style.

In but one example, Malick effectively uses the ambiguity of sound and then later unveils the source of that sound in a kind of slow reveal that links the sound to a particular feeling or motif in such a way that he evokes mystery and awe, not the hyperventilating stimulation so often the norm today in film. Antonioni was extremely effective at the clever use of ambiguity to create a sense of mystery, and Malick, apparently inspired by Antonioni's *Zabriski Point*, uses wind chimes to allude to the mystery of sex to which the young boy (played by Hunter McCracken) is slowly being revealed and later shamefully tries to rid himself of by throwing the nightgown in the river. Once the source of the sound is seen (the wind chimes), and the boy steals the night-gown from his fantasy woman's house, we don't hear the sound again.

[As a side note, the nightgown scene has prompted more Internet searches to my blog than any other topic, and apparently evokes deep, unresolved emotions. Suffice it to say many people are captured by the mystery of the scene and don't understand the boy's subsequent reaction. To me, he is clearly ashamed of creating a sexual fetish *of the nightgown. He tries to hide the gown at first, then washes it down the river—an attempt to dissolve his guilt and shame into an overwhelming natural element that washes away all sins and purifies his conscience as a result. I believe the scene essentially depicts the boy's baptism into sexually-aware manhood. As such, the nightgown evolves from being a fetish to a sacred baptismal shroud.]*

Ambiguity, used sparingly by most filmmakers today, becomes the central stylistic choice in Malick's *Tree of Life*. While most directors and producers are so afraid to alienate or offend an audience who, according to conventional wisdom, can only take things if spelled out literally, Malick assumes his audience is intelligent, and can follow his meandering, poetic connections.

Another example of the effective use of sound is the peaceful and alluring sound the ocean, which bookends the film—beginning with the "spirit image" and ending with the final beach scene, where the various characters meet to reconcile in a timeless, meditative state (all while evoking the films of Frederico Fellini). All of this stuff is so counter to the normal fodder we are fed on television and in film that it is extremely gratifying to find the critical response to *Tree of Life* to be so favorable, although the film did apparently receive some booing at its Cannes premiere (as did Antonioni with some of his films). The film did win the top prize at Cannes, which also helped assuage the critics. My challenge to Fox Searchlight is to go as wide as possible with this film; they might be surprised by the outcome, particularly among a Christian audience.

Tree of Life is built on the use of motifs, used brilliantly with sound and source slowly revealed, cyclic re-occurrence, the grand scale of time being interleaved with the present moment. Malick's particular approach, at least in this film, is more akin to music than the Hollywood style that traces its roots back to D. W. Griffith, kinetic editing and *The Great Train Robbery*. Instead, Malick seems to draw his inspiration from the Bible, surrealists (Bunuel and Dali), Italian neo-realist filmmakers (Fellini and Antonioni), existential science fiction films (Tarkovsky and Kubrick) and the literature of William Faulkner and James Joyce. *Tree of Life* is a grand amalgam of sometimes contradictory influences, including an effusive orchestration from Smetana's *The Moldau*, and yet it reaches beyond these influences even while honoring their undeniable presence.

It is a testament to the encyclopedic scope of the film that one can find various critics not only responding in completely different ways, but referring to completely different sets of (assumed) influences that Malick brought to his film. As such, the film is a Rorschach test of sorts, and one can take from it multiple readings, which I'm sure is Malick's intention, and this shows how powerful his multi-layered ambiguity can be as a storytelling device.

To turn to the thematic elements of *Tree of Life*, I have written in the SolPix webzine and blog about the need for a more "humanistic" media and film and even elaborated further to use the term "spiritual humanism." Malick's film is, I would say, a spiritually humanistic film for several reasons. First, he deals with the subject of the origins and nature of violence and compassion and their relationship to human choice. Second, he seeks a balance between nature and mankind's desire to control nature. Third, he sees reconciliation as the answer to questions of meaning and happiness. Finally, he sees something binding all these threads, or branches, of life together (even an extra-human aspect): love. And this love compels the tree to grow ever outward from its branches. From a biblical perspective, the tree is also a source of knowledge. But the overall energy and essence that drives this movement of life is a love that Malick sees shimmering through the light of his images and characters, of nature, of far-flung galaxies, of the extra-dimensional "non-physical"—in short, the entirety of life itself. While it is generally uncomfortable to discuss an extra-human love in a culture where our obligatory "love you's" are generally restricted to our close familial ties, if we are to believe Malick, the force of love is quite large and behind everything we see in the natural world and beyond. Call this force "God" or whatever name you will, it is tangible as long as we make it so. It is this existential choice to, in essence, *choose and create an alternative to a cold universe*, that takes Mr. Malick beyond Antonioni, who generally only saw despair in his landscapes, and very little hope. From a philosophical perspective, this probably puts Malick closer to the Christian existentialism of Kierkegaard and further from the absurdism and alienation of Camus, who would find better company with Antonioni.

In terms of compassion, it is apparent that Malick sees compassion as one choice among many. This is why the dinosaur scene was so pivotal and important. He is showing us that there is a primal, non-rational (or proto-rational) choice involved in treating others compassionately; that this choice in a sense comes from beyond us, yet does nonetheless express itself in daily human decisions. It is the same choice Mr. Obrien's children make when deciding not to hit their father (played in a *tour de force* performance by Brad Pitt), even as he chides them to do so while he teaches them to box and defend themselves.

As for nature, the imposition of the (male) architecture over the (feminine) natural world is, apparently, the wider tragedy of human existence to date, and a theme clearly traceable to Antonioni's early works. It is the exploration of this "architectural" theme that makes Sean Penn's scenes so important (some critics have suggested they should have been cut). It is the dwarfing of the natural landscape when compared to mankind's architected space—seen through the modern scenes—through which something is lost. This pattern happens as one chooses the path of "nature" (in the negative sense of the will to dominate) over "grace," according to the preamble of the film. The grown son (moodily played by Sean Penn) finds himself dwarfed by his own creation, but he is unhappy because there is no love in his architecture, only utility. He longs for the love of the natural world and of his mother (delicately played by Jessica Chastain) for which he has destroyed in an egoistic attempt at control as he attempts to overcome the (perceived) failings of his father.

Thus the decidedly "male" perspective finds its limits; for on a grander, larger scale, it is mystery—one might say the feminine—still reigns supreme. We cannot "know" reality through the rational mind, just as the natural world cannot ultimately be "tamed" by architecture and science. In truth, we live by grace, or the force of will, depending on your perspective and your choice. But clearly the individual will cannot control the larger, herculean forces of nature. We could, for example, be wiped out in an instant by an errant asteroid. And even if we controlled all the asteroids, some other, larger calamity would rear its head. Thus the great winds of time and space, of galaxies and stars, which provide the context for mankind's "will"—a will that in an attempt to impose itself on nature does so only with a certain folly and arrogance, for nature is, and always has been, the wider context through which we live. Any attempt to control nature in the broadest sense is futile, and if some semblance of this does happen, it only occurs through the mastery achieved through the reconciling power of love—a process Malick refers to as "grace."

Further, Malick seems to argue that love is the natural evolutionary path for mankind. Mankind, stubborn to prove otherwise, continually tries to control through his will (and the proxy servants, science and technology) what cannot ultimately be controlled, but rather must be surrendered to and accepted in order to find peace. Without this surrendering there is only conflict, only suffering. So it is the binding nature of love and reconciliation, as seen at the end of the film as the characters reconcile in timelessness on the beach, returning to the ocean from which they arose—it is here that Malick beckons us toward a path that is separate from the contentiousness of domination and control and toward a more "New Testament" vision of acceptance, surrender and compassion, and Malick asserts that it is through that path that we will find happiness. And again, we are compelled in this direction by the life force itself.

As a bit of personal background, Malick had just released *Days of Heaven* when I was in film school in the early eighties. At that time I was studying European film, with a focus on Antonioni. *Zabriski Point, Blow Up, The Passenger*—all of these films by Antonioni were fresh in my mind. It was nearly twenty years later (in 1998) before Malick would return to film, and nearly twenty years later (in 2000) before I would return to film after a long stint on a different career path outside of film and the arts. Now, decades after the French and American New Wave, Malick returns to re-assert the power of those film artists who apparently impacted many of us so deeply, and to pay homage to the artistic territory they staked out—to extend the branches of the tree they and his life represent.

Malick, as a cinephile and philosophy teacher of a certain age, was certainly impressed in his youth by many of the same directors I was: Kubrick, Antonioni, Godard, Fellini, and so on. It was also these (mostly) Europeans, who had such an impact on the likes of Francis Coppola and Martin Scorsese, who molded my own opinions about the potential for film and film language, and, moreover, how to create a uniquely American aesthetic that nonetheless pays homage to these great European masters who offered us an alternative to the studio film and style. Malick continues that tradition with *Tree of Life*. It's not that all films must conform and be like *Tree of Life*, but certainly our cultural palette must and should include many more films of a similar aesthetic.

Malick, who began his career in the early seventies (with *Badlands*) at roughly the same time as Martin Scorsese, became in a sense our lost master. Again, after *Days of Heaven* he wasn't seen again for 20 years. Thankfully, he has returned to us in full glory. This is a glory that he himself would eschew; for the celebrity he sees is not so much in himself as an artist, but as a vessel of the beauty of life that he sees around him, and a translator and messenger to us of that beauty. While many of our most financially successful filmmakers are more architects than artists—technicians under the employ and influence of more utilitarian forces—Mr. Malick is an artist and a teacher, and, miraculously, one now allowed to express himself in a fairly unrestricted way. Malick may have given us more if he had the chance, but fortunately what we wind up with is his best, for that is what he seems to demand of himself.

We may look back on Mr. Malick's recent work and see it as the beginning of a re-invigorated American art cinema. Suffice it to say that Mr. Malick sees the world through a different, more compassionate lens than the (currently) dominant forces in society and in film. He is leading us toward a new sensibility, and we should follow.

A NEW HUMANISM

(2011)

"Nonviolence means avoiding not only external physical violence but also internal violence of spirit. You not only refuse to shoot a man, but you refuse to hate him." —Martin Luther King, Jr.

When starting my production company in 2000 one of my personal goals was to form a company that produced and promoted "humanistic media." Exactly what that means has been a work in progress, as the term humanism itself can take on a variety of meanings depending on who is defining the term.

Humanists, in the traditional sense, are secular in their outlook. They believe that "people are the center of all things" and that scientific rationality, not religion, superstition or spirituality, offer the best answers for humanity's ills. What I have proposed as defining "humanistic media" is different from the purely secular in that it can and should include what might be called a spiritual or New Humanism, as laid out by the late Mario Rodriquez Cobos or the "common human values" supported by the Dalai Lama in laying the groundwork for World Peace. Moreover, such a humanism can be more inclusive than "faith-based" themes that while inspirational can also have narrow definitions of what kinds of media messages can and should be conveyed, generally involving the acceptance of a Judeo-Christian god. The tenets of such a "New Humanism" include:

1. An acceptance of the intrinsic value of all human beings

2. A realization that humanity is interdependent and shares common values

3. Understanding that there should be a balance between social and individual needs

4. Accepting personal responsibility for the social and physical environment and choosing accordingly

5. Seeing non-violence and reconciliation as a world view that can lead mankind toward peace both individually and collectively.

To many secular humanists, this broader definition of humanism is an impossibility. Any mention of the concept of words such as "interdependence" or "spirit" is an anathema to the Western mind that seeks through rational thought to eliminate the darkness of superstition and religious dogma that has in so many cases burdened humankind.

What I propose, however, is a reconciliation. How so? Rational, secular humanism and the scientific method have led us, in the past century, to theoretical physics. The rise of this New Physics allows us to ponder a multi-dimensional, inter-dependent world. The result is a new world view. That view can lead to a framework of understanding that looks outside of what traditional Western science might term "rational" or "objective." At the end of the day, I believe New Physics will lead us to a world where the scientific and spiritual are reconciled and to conclude that the dualistic notion of "self" and "other" needs to be rethought. At its core, this is what my film *Clouds* is about. The co-producer of *Clouds*, Will Arntz, later explored these ideas in the *What the Bleep* films.

Buddhist traditions in a sense came to similar conclusions as did the New Physicists. The Buddhist philosophers see a world of interdependence, where the autonomous individual self is seen as an illusion. Quantum physics also leads to similar conclusions, where the quantum reality is in a sense shaped by the observer of that reality—the two are seen as a unity that cannot be separated.

The Buddhist mindset will also lead us to the conclusion that the human personality is only a series of "aggregates"—processes—much like traditional Western Science does in breaking down human beings into strictly physical terms. If misinterpreted, both Buddhist analysis and science can lead to a nihilistic view that sees human value systems as ultimately futile. For science, because people are seen through the lens of physical processes, some conclude no value system exists outside of the desire of humankind to construct one. While Buddhist thought has overcome nihilism through self-generated compassion, Western Science generally has no such refuge. To the nihilist, morality is not "natural" but may even stand against natural law, which to the nihilist is often simply the survival of the fittest, motivated by a desire to dominate and overcome nature. To these people, power is the only defining element of life; if emotional attachments are allowed, they are generally familial and sentimental. However, the danger of nihilism is that it can and does lead us down the path, eventually, of social disintegration, as the moral dimension is eschewed for a strictly material view and social cohesion based on ethics, morality and the "golden rule" dissolves. To be clear, it is not usually scientists who create these problems, but people who misinterpret science and see science and technology primarily as vehicles for gain.

In our modern era, nihilism often means that we throw the humanist baby out with the religious bath water. Close behind in the dustbin are nuance, the poetic and the beautiful. As we witness nihilism on parade within our current economic situation, and the corruption apparently evident within the halls of finance, we see blatant examples of actions taken without a moral compass to guide them, or that moral compass is simply a legalistic frame where the individual or businessman seeks only to adhere to the letter of the law (if we're lucky), but sees no social obligation to his fellow human being outside of what he can get away with to exploit and/or manipulate people more effectively. Sometimes this exploitation and manipulation is assisted by the clever misuse of technology. In the extreme, this literally results in an institutionalized pathology. At best, the "meaningless becomes meaningful" as so eloquently stated by one of the interviewees in the documentary film we co-produced with director Ngawang Choephel, *Tibet in Song*. At worst, corporate psychopaths prevail. Clive Boddy has theorized about this kind of corporate pathology and how it could one of the root causes of the financial crisis. To quote Boddy from *The Journal of Business Ethics:*

> Psychopaths, rising to key senior positions within modern financial corporations, where they are able to influence the moral climate of the whole organization and yield considerable power.

While Hollywood may not be run by psychopaths, it may buttress a culture where they can survive. In short, I would relate Wall Street to Hollywood in this sense. Both have constructed machines to generate money that, over time, become self-fulfilling and self-generating. Just as some accuse "primary dealers" on Wall Street of unethically gaming an essentially high-tech closed system, so Hollywood Studios might be seen as gaming the system with special-effects laden blockbuster films that cater to a certain audience, trained one might say to think and feel in a certain way and respond to what is often essentially shallow sensationalism and sentimentality. Once trained, this (generally young) audience returns like lemmings to the next hypnotic film in the lineup. It's not unlike the Romans and the Coliseum. Was it always like this? No. We have degenerated into the current situation over the last thirty years after making some progress in reaction to the immense destruction of World War II.

But is the current situation in the media really that bad? To the crowds at the Cineplex, apparently not. And, unlike the activities of some of our creative financial wizards, at least it is legal. Who am I to spoil all the fun? However, over time, I would argue, there is a cultural corrosion that occurs. Why this occurs is that individuals are trained, from very young, to think and feel within a certain consumer framework that is shallow, selfish, lacks critical thinking, and imbues a general lack of empathy for anyone outside of one's close ties. Moreover, media messages are generally defined within "heroic" stories that are often a melodramatic mockery of the ideals of the hero as put forth in our Western tradition. Such a perversion of the notion of the hero, such a lack of empathy, such a narcissistic over-concern with the individual self and/or the myopic importance of the nuclear family over and above society as a whole, leads to a society that is unsustainable and will eventually fold in on itself in a dark spiral of self-destruction. If you doubt what I say, read the comments on many blogs. See the lack of empathy for the viewpoint(s) raised. See the anger, the hatred. Is this a society that can survive into the future?

Our young people, enveloped in video games, are urged to continue because, according to studies their skills are increased. Per a recent article on NPR's website:

> [S]tudies show that video gamers show improved skills in vision, attention and certain aspects of cognition. And these skills are not just gaming skills, but real-world skills. They perform better than non-gamers on certain tests of attention, speed, accuracy, vision and multitasking...

Not a word here about being a better human being. In fact, the values described above seem more appropriate for a machine. Of course, we don't value the inefficient and contradictory "human" values; rather, it is the utilitarian "skills" acquired for our businesses and military (obviously what is really important) that we value. And video games are certainly cheaper than college.

As for the movies, what may not survive our urge toward utilitarian values is the type of independent film that, as of late, generally expresses humanistic ideals. If funding becomes more difficult for independent film, humanistic voices in media will become fewer and fewer, at least in the mainstream media. And when we see humanistic messages, they are more likely to appear, ironically, in the cartoons from Pixar and Disney. All the better for Wall Street, because these images cannot be generated cheaply and must be controlled by major corporations. Human qualities are apparently expensive to create and only commercially viable when people are turned into digital avatars.

So what would be anti-humanist in its content? In my mind, any film or story that promotes a villain or the "other" as a "bug to be squashed." While this is fun to the adolescent video gamer, it may not be the best model for adult humanistic storytelling. But since our adolescent audiences are often key to modern Cineplex, modern villains and the notion of a mythical evil that can be "terminated" or "removed" so that others can be "happy" (translated to bonding sentimentally with their tribe) leaves us open, in my mind, to a fascistic mindset where we need an "enemy" to unite us, be that a Jew, an Islamic terrorist, an Alien from another planet, an Orc in Middle Earth, or (for the Chinese Government) a Tibetan Nun in a prison camp.

Perhaps this is just the nature of things. Perhaps I am too utopian and naively optimistic in the hope that people can and should live with empathy for one another, to have mutual respect for one another, and to value each human being equally. In other words, to see ourselves in the eyes of the other and to have a culture that expresses those ideals. While I might seem a little serious, these are serious times. Perhaps even too serious for films to really matter anymore—although I continue to hope that's not the case. I'd like to think good films matter now more than ever.

A recent blog debate by Dr. Cornel West and Dr. Robert George (at the time both professors at Princeton) lays out the arguments for a spiritual (in this case Christian) humanism. There could also be a Buddhist Humanism and a Jewish Humanism and an Islamic Humanism. My point is not to convert, but to show the potential within human consciousness to come to a conciliatory stance that looks toward compassion, not endless conflict, as the answer to human ills.

I urge media people to consider these ideas and the give and take between the media and the mass audience. I urge media providers to have a sense of social responsibility towards those to whom they promote their messages. I urge us to move beyond an us/them framework and toward a "we" framework that supports both justice and reconciliation—and will therefore support tolerance and forgiveness—a forgiveness that moves beyond the merely sentimental to the compassionate.

If we do not support this kind of media, be that within our news, our films, our books or our video games, we will continue to see society erode to the point where no compromise is possible, no unity is possible, and only force and fear are recognized as organizing principles of society. Some people in our society might like it that way, but they are not wise in their conclusions.

In my estimation, we must obtain wisdom, and we as media providers can put into the mix of our messages those that support justice with reconciliation and which do not polarize us into camps that cannot agree and cannot move forward into the future. While some may argue that "heroes and villains" are the best framework for storytelling, there are numerous examples of humanistic film that have conflict but do not promote a simplistic us/them viewpoint of the world.

Of those that promote the kind of humanism I describe I would put Cornel West at the top of the list. Dr. West has in fact developed some ideas and themes regarding "non-market values" similar to those outlined in my play *Tibet Does Not Exist* as well as the nature of compassion described by the Dalai Lama. I personally would give these ideas a chance and listen, as academic and spiritual leaders such as Cornel West and the Dalai Lama provide ideas that can offer an alternative to the endless wars, economic and social injustice, and lack of unity that we find today. Taken into media and art, they provide an alternative to nihilism, cynicism, and general lack of faith in our common future and instead give us a much-needed vision of hope.

WAKE UP TIME FOR AMERICA

(SPRING, 2011)

"Peace is a big thing... it is not just the absence of armed conflict. Peace is socio-economic justice, gender equality—a world where people live with freedom from fear, freedom from want." —Jody Williams

Since the 1970s, after the end of the Bretton woods financial era (AKA, gold-backed dollar system) there has been an accelerating decline of the Middle Class in this country. The graph below shows the discrepancy between rich and poor in the U.S. as of 2007, a trend that has only accelerated since the financial collapse of 2008.

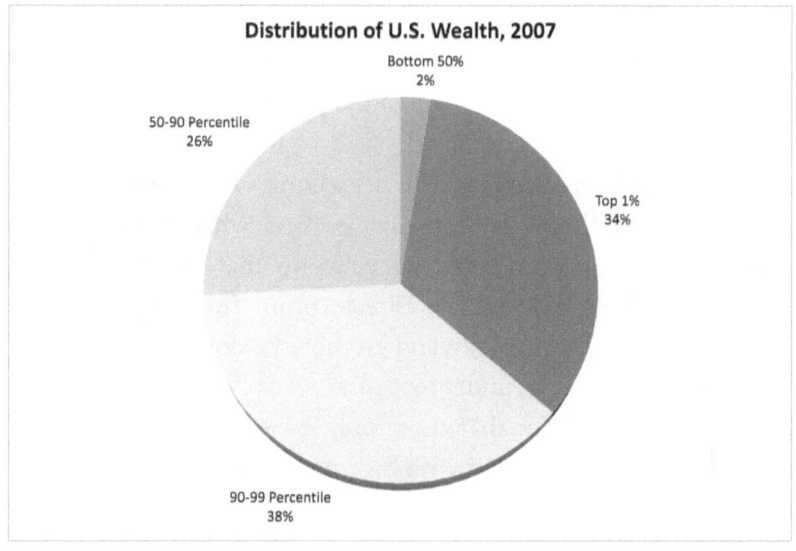

(Source: "Ponds & Streams: Wealth and Income in the U.S., 1989 to 2007").

CNN sums up the current situation as follows:

> The richest one-percent of US Households had a net worth 225 times greater than that of the average American household in 2009, according to analysis conducted by the Economics Policy Institute, a liberal think tank. That's up from the previous record of 190 times greater, which was set in 2004.

Why has this inequality happened? In addition to the standard response that we've "shipped all of our jobs overseas," or "Americans have spent beyond their means," another reason this shift has occurred is to a large extent because the fruits of the productivity gains made in our modern economies have shifted disproportionately to the upper 10% of society. To put it another way, Americans should be making more money for their labor relative to the increased productivity we've seen in the past 30 years. According to Robert Reich in his book *Aftershock:*

> [Americans have] not kept up with what the larger economy could and should have been able to provide them. [During the last 30 years] the American economy had been growing briskly, and America's Middle Class naturally expected to share in that growth. But it didn't. A larger and larger portion of the economy's winnings had gone to the people at the top.

None of this has happened in a vacuum. Government policies dating back to Jimmy Carter have evolved what *Foreign Affairs* magazine called a "winner take all" economy that has weakened labor organizations, allowed the élite to profit from the misuse of de-regulation and technology, and promoted a slow drift away from the gains made by labor under 1930s and 1960s New Deal and Great Society legislation. Not that those policies were perfect; but compared to what we have now, with income inequality in the U.S. approaching that of a third world nation, we certainly need to rethink what we have lost. According to *Foreign Affairs,* this policy drift was a very deliberate and well-funded effort by wealthy and conservative forces to turn back the clock. The results are now bearing fruit.

In addition to issues with labor displacement, productivity and bad policy, speculative finance capitalism (newly unleashed by the de-regulation of the last 10 years) allows the creation of bubbles that serve to shift enormous amounts of wealth to a small percentage, while the bulk of others are left holding the speculative bag. Moreover, there is overwhelming evidence that the "primary dealers" on Wall Street are improperly gaming the system (through practices such as High Frequency Trading) to the detriment of many.

More recently, the Federal Reserve's policy of "quantitative easing" (AKA "money printing" as U.S. debt is bought outright by the Fed) has fueled world inflation, particularly in energy, food and other commodities. This impacts not only the American Middle Class, but large swaths of society around the globe. Some would argue that the uprisings in North Africa and the Middle East are to a large part due to inflation, indirectly influenced by the Fed's actions. While the Middle East's move toward democracy is positive, the underlying issues of inflation will remain once political change occurs—that is, unless economic reforms are put in place as well.

The challenge is this: how do we distribute wealth in a just and fair way so that the productive gains made by society are distributed fairly across society? And how do we do so in a way that doesn't undermine our belief in liberty and democracy?

First, we must look at the idea of Economic Justice, which is separate and distinct from socialism—a word so many use to describe any policy aimed at distributing wealth.

According to the late Mortimer J. Adler, justice is part of the three pillars of any democratic society that includes justice, liberty, and equality. In our society, liberty—and more precisely a libertarian ideal of liberty—has taken precedence over equality and justice. In reality, according to Adler, all three ideas buttress and are necessary for the others to survive.

The liberties that we have remaining are due to the fact that the upper 1% still needs liberty to do what they need to do to exploit the lower 99%. But on analysis, liberty taken to its extreme is, according to Adler, not liberty but license. License arises when liberty is used to exploit others in a way that is neither equitable nor just.

In Greece, France, the UK and other countries, we are seeing large-scale protests and rioting, all fueled by questions regarding fundamental justice and fairness arising from the financial crisis and the resulting "austerity" programs. Many feel that the EU's economic bailouts of the banks have come with austerity measures that unjustly punish people at large, while banks are provided ample funds and support by the European Central Bank. To more and more Europeans, the question of economic justice is very much on their minds. It is no small irony that the country where democracy was founded (Greece) should suffer inordinately under the boot of finance capitalism, and that Greece may be where democracy rises yet again.

The timing couldn't be better. The rise of authoritarian capitalism in China as a model for the future, and (some would argue) the corollary rise of Homeland Security in this country, are aimed at dismantling the pillar of liberty that the upper 1% see as the final roadblock to financial utopia. In other words, at some point in the future, the top 1%, who live everywhere and nowhere by virtue of their wealth, could literally "buy" liberty within the global economy, while the rest of us have either no liberties (outside of the "liberty" to consume), or will see those liberties erode. We cannot let this happen.

What is the answer? The answer is simple. We must re-introduce the ideas of equality and justice into our economic sphere. This can happen in a number of ways, to be sure, some incremental, and some radical. And while incremental (some would say "band aid") solutions are proposed in Congress every day, we will eventually most likely need radical shifts in our economic structures over the longer term. This is because we have let the situation devolve to such an extent that merely cutting discretionary spending and raising taxes, along with other incremental solutions, will not get us where we need to go. Moreover, these incremental solutions usually saddle most of us with a burden that should be equally distributed among all.

Many on the more intelligent financial blogs, including *Zero Hedge, Seeking Alpha, Max Keiser* and others, can lead the way toward a more equitable financial situation, but in my opinion the majority of those blogs, while often brilliant at analyzing the fundamental problems, generally do not put forward workable solutions. Any solutions so far have been more rage-based actions and lashing out (the recent "crash JP Morgan" campaign is an example). While crashing J.P. Morgan may provide some emotional release, it doesn't solve our long term problems, and may just indeed cause more suffering.

A commentator in *Naked Capitalism* put it this way:

It seems like we've come full circle back to where we were in the latter part of the 19th century. We did not learn, or we've completely forgotten, the lessons of the events of the first half of the 20th century taught us.

And where those events eventually led were to global conflict and World War II. And we seem very much on that path in the Middle East, where continued conflict could certainly spin out of control and involve Iran and Israel.

But rather than war, what we need is global currency cooperation, and probably a world reserve or trade currency (with its value linked to gold) that all others are indexed against. Economists such as Joseph Stiglitz have in fact supported such an idea, and the IMF (to the chagrin of some) has proposed using their Special Drawing Rights (SDRs) for this purpose. Once such a new reserve currency was established, participating currencies could be revalued *vis-a-vis* the new world currency in order to tackle trade imbalances. To be economically just, such a new world trade currency would need to be administered in a transparent, democratic way and under a charter that demands it to promote the general welfare, not protect the interests of the few.

In tandem, a world minimum wage (and higher minimum wages

in developed countries) should be established as part of the process. This would allow some of the wage advances that labor should have seen in the last 30 years due to productivity gains to be realized. We must also realize that the question of minimum wage is not only an economic one, but a moral one. For a laborer in Bangladesh (or elsewhere) to make less than 50 cents an hour is immoral and tantamount to slavery.

Further, debt jubilees and/or restructuring should be implemented to allow for many of the world's debts to be either absolved; as a side note, we should avoid ultra long-term bonds to solve the problem, as such techniques just kick the can down the road to as yet unborn generations who might actually try to redeem those instruments. Finally, where possible, minimum income guarantees or a reverse income tax can help the elderly, unemployed and poor stay out of poverty while simplifying our social safety nets; eventually a citizen's dividend could empower both the poor and middle class as well.

As for a world currency, many will cringe at the idea of the IMF creating it, because the danger of any new world currency and probably an associated world central bank would be that it would remain under control of the current banking oligarchs. Believe me, the need for a new world currency has been heatedly discussed in the back rooms of conferences and think tanks (and has probably been agreed upon as the general, consensus direction by the G20), but it must now be done so openly, and in a way that the common person understands the trade-offs. To keep the global financial priesthood in place is not the way forward. We must all, in essence, become economically savvy—or at least enough of us to guide elections intelligently.

A new world currency based on the IMF's SDRs will, many argue, only lead us closer to a centralized world government. But the alternative to some kind of cooperative currency system (whether it be based on the IMF or not) is a step into isolationism, hyper localism and nationalism. In my opinion this would be counterproductive—particularly if global banking institutions and corporations remained intact as local and national governments were weakened by their inevitable insolvencies. This is one of the key weaknesses to the libertarian's vision of the future. Indeed, such a future as envisioned by the Ron Pauls of the world could lead to a neo-feudal world of corporate control. One could, in theory, devolve both government and corporate power in tandem, but this is unlikely to happen and is unrealistic in today's modern age. Assuming global financial institutions and corporations remain, they would be able to game the system with no adequate force to counter them (i.e., strong central governments) should further economic collapse occur (and it likely will). Again, the result could be neo-feudalism and much more inequality than is seen today. In short, we need some form of global governance, but of a flavor that reflects the general welfare, not the exigencies of the global élite. It's my belief that the Internet could be a vehicle for such governance (and perhaps even a people-based financial system—a kind of People's World Bank—linked to it), where people are organized via the Internet in as yet un-defined methods (i.e., Internet Unions)—something like large scale, global "MoveOn.org's." The catch is that such governance must have the force of law as well as influence—and we are a long way from that. Moreover, so-called "kill switches" for the Internet and telecommunications would need to be universally banned. But again, without some kind of global governance we would risk regressing into a modern feudalism as Western central governments weakened due to economic upheaval and (likely) capitulation to the financial élites, with corporate fiefdoms becoming the modern equivalent of the feudal Lords and Castles of the past (apparently the *Earthseed* books are a chilling premonition of such a world). What we need instead is a united front, organized globally via the Internet, that allows for localities to make a consistent and unified stand against globalism.

In summary, we need to rework world finances so that they align with democratic values, and do so in a cooperative way that recognizes that people need to organize locally but have a global reach, because it is not rational to do otherwise. It is irrational for the top 1% to continue to hold the bottom 99% hostage because they are able to create effective propaganda that labels any attempt to introduce economic equality and justice as "socialistic," and are able to use global infrastructure and organizations such as the World Trade Organization (WTO) to undermine human rights and environmental policies using a "divide and conquer" strategy.

Further, it is not rational because the wealthy will in fact be, over the long term, much better off if their wealth is correctly revalued and/or taxed down to reflect equity, and the wages of workers are correctly valued up to accurately reflect the gains of greater overall productivity. Believe me, the wealthy can continue to prosper in the new, more equitable, world financial system moving forward, but in a balanced way. Moreover, the promises made in the past of "increased leisure and abundance" due to the miracles of technology will finally be achieved, and the wealthy will then rise with the rest of us, but all in tandem in a manner that reflects economic justice. Thus would the three democratic pillars of liberty, justice and equality be realized in the economic sphere.

We must all do what we can to educate ourselves and others that this is not only doable, but necessary for our common survival. This, in combination with aggressive moves on the environmental and energy front, can move us into this century without the wars, social strife, and pollution seen in the past. Further, we can avoid the police-state tactics that so many are beginning to see as inevitable if we suffer another major economic collapse; we must fight these fascist tendencies with absolute vigor. Once a more equitable world financial system is in place, and capital is freed up by debt jubilees, currency revaluation and military downsizing, we could intelligently "quantitative ease" (using debt-free currency where possible) in such a way as to develop a world economy that is sustainable environmentally, and hires millions to do the job of building the sustainable infrastructure of the future.

While I'm not an economist, I offer these suggestions as one who has worked in the financial world and studied both the history of democracy and economics. In my mind, true liberty cannot exist without justice, and that includes justice in our economic system. And while some may find these ideas Pollyannaish, the alternative is a new dark age, and we can't allow that to happen.

A WORLD WITHOUT WAR

(2006)

"Forgiveness is not always easy. At times, it feels more painful than the wound we suffered, to forgive the one that inflicted it. And yet, there is no peace without forgiveness." —Marianne Williamson

As war has apparently been with human beings since they were first able to hoist a rock and throw it in anger at a neighboring tribe, it's hard to imagine a world without war. Like language, war seems an indelible part of the human experience. Yet, if there was ever a time in the history of the planet to organize an effort to end war as an institution, now is that moment. While many would view the world today as an increasingly dangerous place, according to the *Human Security Report* published by Oxford University Press, global conflicts have actually decreased significantly since the end of the Cold War, with 40% fewer armed conflicts in 2003 compared to 1992. To be sure, the overwhelming obstacles to peace presented by the Cold War have been replaced by more subtle (some would say insidious) exigencies of the corporate-warrior state, where a pervasive and persistent War on Terror very neatly supplies the political élites with an organizing principle. But still, like the Cold War, these obstacles can be overcome. The work is certainly difficult, if not multi-generational. Those that began the effort would probably not live long enough to see its fruits.

The fundamental question surrounding war is: why? There are several reasons for war, all intertwined and interleaved in a vast social, personal, political syndrome, not unlike a complex illness for which there is no one cause, no one cure, and no sure prognosis. But if we turn toward the individual human being as a starting place, it is there that any effort to ban war may find its most likely success. For it is on the level of the individual—how each person interacts with their fellow human beings—that the seeds of war begin. It is in individual hatred, biases, bigotries, selfishness, and sentiment that the drive for war takes root. It is therefore in raising individual consciousness about the ultimate fallacy of war and its institutions, about its self-perpetuating nature and the tendency of the politicians who support war to deceive through propaganda, manipulation and emotion—it is through an effort to raise human consciousness (or at least raise the consciousness of enough people to make policy change) that an effort toward world peace can take shape.

The obstacles are daunting: a thoroughly entrenched, multi-billion dollar military industrial complex that serves as a *de facto* jobs program because "national defense" is an area where most can agree funds should be spent; politicians and policy makers who have convinced themselves that there is a persistent international conspiracy (whether communist or socialist or terrorist) against "good" that will always achieve a response, even if that response is disproportionate to the threat and ineffective as a deterrent; a sense that some individuals will only respond to force, and that if free societies don't understand this reality that they will be taken by force and subjected to tyranny; individual human beings who believe that some people are inherently evil and malevolent, with evil intentions often fueled by satanic influences; human beings that believe that their particular brand of religion is the only valid one, and that people who believe otherwise are inherently of less value; wealthy individuals who value property above people, and who will quickly sacrifice the later for the former; and a consistent and pervasive desire for human beings to dehumanize themselves in a variety of ways in order to take away the painful awareness of their own mortality, and thus trivializing the deaths associated with war, unless those deaths are within their own sphere.

In other words, the current political institutions and structure, social mindset, economic reality and overwhelming precedence of history work against a world devoid of war. War has become a way, a method of being, an economic force, and an emblem of democratic strength. War has even become integrated into consumer culture, where aggression, pride, guile, greed and selfishness are trumped up by the media as values worthy of a modern democratic society. Apparently aggression is the only sufficient fuel (along with oil) for capitalist progress, which promotes individual strength over communal good, and values the symbols and rhetoric of freedom (the "freedom brand" you might say) more than freedom itself. At the same time, an aggressive materialist society ignores the individual struggle—often more emotional, spiritual and psychological in nature—required to secure freedom as it focuses on the often shallow requirements of consumer and economic freedom.

Now some of these "aggressive" values may even be beneficial, and some have already found adequate channels of expression through sports, entrepreneurship, and healthy debate devoid of guile. But too often the expression of aggressive behavior, particularly in the United States, is becoming commodified to such an extent that it becomes a part of the culture in such a way that makes it much easier to manipulate people into war and toward policies that promote a conservative, war-promoting agenda.

And yet if you were to ask most people if they supported the concept of "world peace" they would say unequivocally "yes."

To understand our current situation, it's really necessary to look back to World War II, when the modern military was formed. The doctrine of American military became "overwhelming force" where the sheer ability of American industry to out-produce its enemies became the operating mindset for decades to follow. Certainly it was the credo of the Cold War, where the U.S. military produced enough nuclear warheads to destroy the planet several times over. In this sense adherence to the principle of overwhelming force, while successful in WW II, began to show signs of neurosis during the Cold War and is now showing signs of a full catatonic break with reality during the War on Terror—an effort which requires a completely different doctrine than "overwhelming force" to ensure its long-term success. The War in Iraq is in essence the last insane gasp of the doctrine of overwhelming force (and its bastard child, "smart force", now using killer drones that usually have significant collateral damage), and shows how thoroughly inadequate and delusional it has become as a method for securing democratic goals. Even if we "win" in Iraq, it is unclear if democracy will survive, and whether new conflicts will arise in its wake.

The new method of "war" if you will should be to effectively wage non-violence on a massive and institutional level. To promote, educate and enlighten individuals as to the value of each person and the value of each culture, and to the rights of people to live in peace conduct their lives as they best see fit. In other words, the billions that are spent on the military machine should be largely channeled toward efforts at common human understanding. NGOs, ranging from the Red Cross to Oxfam to the Carter Center—as well as the relevant U.N. agencies—should receive massive funding to eliminate poverty and promote common human respect and decency. While this effort will not work overnight, and may well experience many failures in the short term, over several generations we will see results.

The obstacles to this approach are also numerous. For one, many people feel that the idea that all human beings are inherently of value is an anathema—for whether Christian or Muslim or Jew, it seems that the idea of a "chosen few" is well entrenched, and that for this reason it is easy enough to see people outside of one's own faith as evil, as the enemy or as infidels. According to many of these people, the goals of world peace are "secular humanist" in nature and thus patently evil, undermining national sovereignty to boot. Moreover, if these individuals work for the military industry or have family in the military, the military is a means of economic security for them. A powerful combination of sentiment, religion and economic incentive make it incredibly easy for cynical politicians and profit hungry arms producers to manipulate vast swaths of people in ways that promote war and make it difficult to wage non-violence. In fact, non-violence as a dominant world view is so far from reality today that it seems laughable to think of it as one day being potentially the overwhelming *leitmotif* of human existence. And yet the same thing was said of slavery, or women's rights, and of environmental protections in their day; but slavery has ended, women's rights have made great strides, and environmental protections, while very much a work in progress, have become a reality. Moreover, if you were to ask most people today if they support the concept of "non-violence" they would respond with an overwhelming "yes."

So the answer to the question "how do we create a world without war?" begins today, with our individual choices. Do we act aggressively when it might be more mature and effective to act differently? Do we support organizations that support peace? Do we vote for politicians that have at least the beginnings of an agenda for peace? Do we educate our children in ways that are conducive to peace? Do we seek means and methods to engage in healthy debate with those that disagree with a peace agenda? In other words, do we, and more importantly you as an individual, take the passion for your convictions into your daily life, and not just roll over and play dead whenever challenged about your ideas on peace? Maybe you should finally sign up with a peace organization you've been considering. In other words, maybe you should take some responsibility for peace, both on a spiritual, political, individual and social level, and promote it in a way that manifests peace in your schools, your neighborhood, and your community.

It is here that the "yeses" to world peace will begin. And it is here that the beginnings of a world without wars can take shape.

ACKNOWLEDGMENTS

Several people were instrumental in providing both the means and inspiration to write these essays. Mike Neff, founder and editor-in-chief at the WebDelSol Media complex, is at the top of the list. Mike nudged me into the role of writing political essays for *The Potomac Journal*, something I really would not have considered had he not suggested it. That said, I'm grateful he did. Roughly half of the essays in this volume originated from that webzine.

In terms of the physical production of the book, I have to thank Ander Monson, John McTague, "Jenny" at First Editing, Michael Campbell, Mike Neff and my wife Diana, all who provided the necessary expertise to make this volume the best it could be.

As for any ability to think critically about media and culture, I have to thank my professors at UCLA's film and television critical studies program, including Howard Suber, Janet Bergstrom, Steven Mamber, and Nicholas Browne. Among those able minds, few stand out as mentors more than Howard Suber, professor emeritus with UCLA's film and television program. Howard was incredibly encouraging and was instrumental in helping me gain confidence in my critical writing and understand what it means to be an independent thinker outside of academic conventions.

The Dalai Lama, as an important spiritual mentor to me, has also been a key influence on my thinking. Having had the privilege of experiencing several of his teachings, and read many of his books, I must say he is one of the most open minded people I have ever encountered. I truly believe he and the Tibetans have enabled a world revolution of perception. It is the sad irony of the tragic history of Tibet; for the Tibetan's loss of a homeland has benefitted the world in untold ways. That said, it is incumbent upon us all to hope and pray for a free Tibet.

Another spiritual mentor to me has been Mario Rodriquez Cobos (AKA Silo), whose little book *Humanize the Earth* emblazoned in me a singular purpose. While I never met Silo, and only read one of his books, that book in many ways shaped my beliefs. I must thank Godi Guiterrez for sending me *Humanize the Earth* in the late nineties.

Other spiritual teachers, including Frederick Lenz, Namkha Drimed Rinpoche, Khempo Yurmed Tinly Rinpoche, Yogananda, and others, were also key to how I formed my view of the world. I thank them all.

Finally, I must again thank my wife of over twenty-five years, Diana. As a friend, confident, editor, critic, encourager, and refuge from all things negative, she has continually reminded me that one of the key things that convinced her to marry me was the film-related essays I wrote while at UCLA. It is likely one of the few cases where essays and term papers helped enable a marriage, not jeopardize it.

ABOUT D.R. THOMPSON

D.R. (Don) Thompson is an award-winning filmmaker/producer, acclaimed playwright, and essayist. As a political editor and contributor with *The Potomac Journal* since 2004, Thompson has written numerous essays on a variety of social and political issues, including the financial meltdown, media consolidation, economic inequality, impacts of globalization, Exopolitics/disclosure and the military-industrial complex. Thompson's socially-relevant plays have been staged from Coast-to-Coast in New York, Los Angeles, and the metro DC area and been positively reviewed in *The New York Times, Los Angeles Times, Baltimore Sun* and others. Through his production company nextPix, Thompson has produced, co-produced or co-funded numerous feature films dealing with a variety of humanitarian and social issues, many of which have screened at major film festivals such as Sundance, Hot Docs, Movies that Matter, New York Indie International, Chicago Documentary, Montreal and others. His film *Clouds* (co-produced by the producer of the *What the Bleep* films) was one of the first films to deal with New Physics, won awards and special recognition at 6 film festivals, and was distributed theatrically and on DVD by IN Pictures and Passion River Films. The documentary *Tibet In Song*, co-produced by Thompson with director Ngawang Choephel, won 10 international film awards including a Special Jury Prize at the Sundance Film Festival, the International Human Rights Film Award from Cinema for Peace, and is now available on DVD through New Yorker Films. Thompson is also a 30-year meditator who has studied with a variety of Tibetan and American spiritual masters.

DEL SOL PRESS, based out of Washington, D. C., publishes exemplary and edgy fiction, poetry, and nonfiction (mostly contemporary, with the occasional reprint). Founded in 2002, the press sponsors two annual competitions:

THE DEL SOL PRESS POETRY PRIZE is a yearly booklength competition with a January deadline for an unpublished book of poems.

THE ROBERT OLEN BUTLER FICTION PRIZE is awarded for the best short story, published or unpublished. The deadline is in November of each year.

HTTP://WEBDELSOL.COM/DSP

www.ingramcontent.com/pod-product-compliance
Lightning Source LLC
Chambersburg PA
CBHW031413210526
45464CB00005B/1870